54 Golden Nuggets

The Best of the Telephone Doctor:
Quick Tips to Cure Your
Business Communication Ills

Nancy Friedman
The Telephone Doctor

Published by: HRD Press, Inc.
22 Amherst Road
Amherst, MA 01002
413-253-3488
800-822-2801 (U.S. and Canada)
413-253-3490 (fax)
www.hrdpress.com

ISBN 978-1-59996-255-9

Editorial services by Sally M. Farnham
Production services by Jean Miller
Cover design by Eileen Klockars

Contents

Telephone Service Tips

Table of Contents

Human Resources Tips

Voice Mail, E-Mail, and Cell Phone Tips

Foreword

With thanks to all who read and enjoy this!

Sincerely,

Nancy Friedman

Preface

Throughout my Telephone Doctor career, many of our articles have been reprinted and published in hundreds of newspapers, magazines, and corporate publications. Many of our articles went out to all of our clients and potential clients in our newsletters.

This book is a compilation of over 50 of what we feel (and actually saw) were our most popular and requested articles. It was difficult to decide which articles to put into this book, as any author will tell you; articles are like children, we like them all. And so it is with these.

We hear a lot of comments, letting us know how simple and common sense our articles are. That was my mission, to write for the masses so that anyone who picked up an article could say, "Hey, this is good old common sense information." That's what Telephone Doctor is all about—common sense. However, we always wonder, if it's so common why isn't everyone doing it. So common, but not common sense, I guess?

Okay, that covers the story of how the book came into being.

Throughout the book we have also included some frustrations of the American public. In our request for "What is your perception of rude behavior?" we received hundreds of responses. We've included only the top 10 from each category. Trust me, there are many more.

Now I get to thank the people who helped me. And like most authors, there were many. A few need to be specially mentioned, as they did a lot of the prep and post work on this book.

Valerie Phillips, the best executive assistant anyone could have in the whole world. And NO, you cannot have her.

Dick, my favorite husband. Oh, right, my only one. He has patiently guided me through so many challenges and supported each and every idea and article ever written by me. Thank you! (And no, you can't have him either!)

To my family—David and his wife Robyn; Linda and her husband, Les Steinberg, along with all the grandkids—thank you for everything! (Okay, I'll name them—Ben, Alex, Sami, Lou, and Nina.)

And to our entire Telephone Doctor staff, more thank yous!

Enjoy!

Customer Service Tips

5 Common Threads of Customer Service

The Telephone Doctor surveys show that there are five common threads in customer service, and they are not all good. Below are the big five common threads that can hurt your business.

1 Customers won't go back.

Most customers put a big red "X" on the company.

2 Customers have the memory of an elephant.

Most customers don't forget...ever!

3 Stunned silence.

Most customers can't believe the poor service they have had.

4 Customers will tell all who will listen.

It's free advertising. Unfortunately, it's the wrong kind.

5 Customers LOVE to vent.

Most customers like to get the bad experience off their chest. It's almost cathartic.

Don't let your customers *vent* about you.

5 Ways to Sabotage Your Business

Believe it or not, there are many, many ways to sabotage your business. And, chances are, your staff is doing some of these now, without your even knowing it. And worse yet, you've probably even heard some of this yourself (ouch!). That's the bad news.

The good news is, through our many Telephone Doctor surveys, we're able to bring to you the top five sabotage practices and then show you how to neutralize the effects. So, get ready. You and your staff are about to be in a much better position to handle a situation in which someone says one of the following sabotaging statements:

1 "It's not our policy."

This, unfortunately, is used more as an excuse than anything else. It's a sure thing that the employee has not been shown how to explain a policy to someone. This phrase is used more as something to say when the employee doesn't know what to say. The customer then calls that an excuse.

When customers hear "it's not our policy," they immediately respond (usually silently) with, "Who cares?" What a business needs to understand is, no one but the company's management and staff care about your policies. Do you really think customers say to themselves as they enter or call your place of business, "Gee, I wonder what their policy is on this issue?"

All this being said, there are companies that do have policies that make it more difficult to work with them than with others. So here's a suggestion: Decide on your policy and then work with your staff to find a positive way to explain it to the customer. Otherwise, it will be the customer's policy not to do business with you!

2 "It's not my department."

Well, then whose department is it? Let's remember one of the Telephone Doctor mottos: Tell the customer what you do, not what you *don't* do. If someone mistakenly calls your extension and asks for something that you don't handle, the following is far more effective than saying it's not your department: "Hi, I work in the paint department. Let me get you to someone in the area you need." Don't say, "*You* have the wrong department." Take full responsibility with the "I" statement.

3 "My computer is down."

Yeah, yeah, yeah. We've all heard that one. And Ouch! that one hurts because there are still many customers who remember the days *before* the computer. My goodness, how did we ever survive? Sure it's easier to have the computer, but, believe it or not, millions of businesses were launched and operated on 3" x 5" cards or some other type of manual database.

When your computer crashes, this sounds so much better when responding to a customer request: "I'll be delighted to help you...it may take a little longer as I'll need to do things by hand...our computers are currently down." By saying this, you've still explained what happened, and they'll have a little more compassion as you've offered assistance and didn't simply blame the computer for your inability to help.

4 **"I wasn't here that day" (or "I was on vacation when that happened").**

This one personally really makes me laugh. I don't remember asking them if they were there that day. Does that excuse the company? Do you really think customers care if you weren't here when their problem happened? Honestly, they don't, so it's not even an issue to discuss. Just hit the problem head on—apologize without telling them where you were or weren't. Remember, you *are* the company in the customer's eyes whether you were at work or on vacation when the issue occurred.

5 **"I'm new."**

So? Okay, you're new. Now what? Does being new allow you to be anything but super to the customer? When customers hear this sabotaging statement, do you really think they say, "Oh, so you're new? So that's why I'm getting bad service? Well, then, that's okay...you're new...no problem."

Yes, even if you are new, the customer honestly believes you should know everything about your job. Here's the Telephone Doctor method on this one: You can tell the customer, "Please bear with me, I've only been here a few weeks." That will buy you time. For whatever reason, hearing the short *length* of time you have been with the company means more to the customer than "I'm new." Again, it's more of an excuse. Remember to state the length of time. It's a credibility enhancement. "I'm new" is a credibility buster.

Don't be a "saboteur."

7 Steps to Service Recovery

Almost anyone who's been in a customer service position has run into either an irate caller or person, or a situation that, shall we say, is not pleasant. And even though it may not even be our fault, we still need to know how to recover the situation. Here are the Telephone Doctor's 7 Steps to Service Recovery that will help make your day a better one!

1 It *is* your responsibility. If you have answered the phone on behalf of the company, you have indeed accepted 100% responsibility. At least that's what the caller/customer believes. So get off the "it's not my fault" syndrome, and get on with the "what can I do for you?" position.

2 "I'm sorry" *does* work. Every once in a while, I hear from CSRs who tell me they don't feel they should say "I'm sorry" when it wasn't their fault. Well, as stated above, in the customer's mind, it is your fault. Saying you're sorry won't fix the problem, but it definitely does help to defuse it immediately. Try it. You'll see.

3 Empathize immediately. When someone is angry or frustrated with your company, the one thing they need is someone to agree with them, or at least feel they're being understood. Be careful, though: "I know how you feel" is *not* a good thing to say unless you have been through exactly what the customer has experienced. Try: "That's got to be so frustrating" or "What an unfortunate situation."

4 **Immediate** action is necessary to make a service recovery. Don't make customers wait for good service. Get whatever it is they need to them immediately. Use overnight service if necessary. That's recovery. **Remember the Telephone Doctor's motto:** It should never take two people to give good customer service.

5 Ask what would make customers happy. In a few rare cases, the customer can be a most difficult one. If you have tried what you considered "everything," simply ask the customer, "What can I do to make you happy, Mr. Jones?" In most cases, it may be something you are able to do. You just may not have thought of it. So go ahead and ask them.

6 Understand the true meaning of service recovery. Service recovery is not just fixing the problem. It's making sure it won't happen again. It's listening to the customer. It's going above and beyond.

7 **Follow up.** After you feel the problem has been fixed, follow up. After you've made the customer happy, make an extra phone call a day or so later. Be sure to ask the customer: "Have we fixed everything for you? What else can we do for you?" Be sure the customer is satisfied. When you hear: "Thanks, you've done a great job. I appreciate it," then you know you've achieved service recovery!

"You may be right" is a great service recovery statement.

9 Ways to Gain the Competitive Edge

Tight economy! Reduced staff! Demanding customers!

These days it's extra challenging to satisfy and keep customers. It's even more important than ever because customer loyalty is generally considered the primary engine today to retain sales levels and gain an advantage over the competition. It's been this way for a long time; it's just getting more attention now.

There are hundreds of ways to do better. Here are nine of the most effective:

1 **Know your products and services...inside and out.**
Dealing with an employee who is not knowledgeable frustrates customers. An uneducated employee is semi-useless to a customer. Job knowledge is key in any position. If for any reason your company doesn't offer job knowledge training, make it your own priority to find out as much as you can. Job knowledge is a key ingredient to serving customers.

2 **Believe in your product and services 150 percent.** We know of a salesperson who never had any formal sales training; yet because of his belief in the product/service and his contagious enthusiasm, this person is a top producer in sales. Customers love to buy from salespeople who get excited about their product. Customer service reps are salespeople!

3 **Walk the walk, talk the talk, and practice what you preach.** A Ford employee would not drive any type of car other than a Ford. They would show confidence in their product. Employees need to support their company's products or services before they can expect their customers to have confidence in them.

4 **Keep your word.** Companies spend thousands, sometimes millions of dollars advertising their products and services. They tell the customer they are "the best," "the only," "the number one." "We guarantee our work" isn't enough. Customers need to know that you'll do what you and your advertising say you will. If you claim to provide "the best of something," make sure you keep your word. And be sure all employees keep their word. Telling a customer something will be to them in seven working days, and then missing that deadline is a credibility buster.

5 **Return all calls and e-mails.** It boggles my mind when a call or an e-mail is not returned. There's not an excuse in the world I could buy when that happens. Sure, some of us get way too many calls and aren't able to return them in a timely manner. If that happens to you, have the call returned on your behalf! Not returning an e-mail? How much time does that take? Even if you don't have an answer to the person's question, get back to them letting them know that you are working on it and when approximately you'll get back to them with an answer.

6 **Don't ever forget "who brought you to the dance."** In other words, there are always customers who were with you from the start. They helped make your business a success. They believed in you. A nice simple note once in a while is an ego booster to them and you'll feel good about it, too.

7 **Make "no ulterior motive" calls or notes.** Every once in a while, drop a note or make a phone call to customers (and prospective customers) without trying to "sell" them something. The Telephone Doctor labels those "no ulterior motive" calls. They're "just because" calls...and are well received. When was the last time you heard from a salesperson or a company just to say "Hi"? (See what I mean?)

8 **Be in a good mood...all the time!** When customers leave or hang up the phone after speaking with you, they should think to themselves, "That was a great visit/call." Not in a good mood? Learn how to be. Remember one of the Telephone Doctor mottos: "A phony smile is better than a real frown." Do you really think the first runner-up of the Ms. America contest is as "thrilled for the winner" as she says or shows she is? Talk about a great big phony smile!

9 **Participate in customer service training programs at your business.** Sure, you know how to be a good CSR, but everyone could use a refresher. And if there are no programs on customer service offered at your work, ask for them. At best, you'll be ahead of the competition, and at worst, you'll at least be even with them. Customer service is not a department. It is a philosophy. And it's for the entire company. Everyone needs to embrace it—or it doesn't work.

Follow any one of these to gain your competitive edge.

10 Best Customer Service Techniques

Most of us think we're pretty good at customer service. We get up in the morning...get ready for our jobs...drive to the office...get a parking space—sometimes close in, sometimes far out—walk into the office...grab a cup of coffee...sit down at our desk...and then: ring, ring, ring. Our phones start. It's usually a customer. If you're in the customer service business (and who isn't these days?), whether it's for external or internal customer service, your day is spent trying to please someone. Somehow, we're *all* customers in one way or another. I've been training corporations on customer service for many years and during that time have found out what the customer likes best. Here are our Telephone Doctor's 10 Best Customer Service Techniques. By using just one of them, you're bound to see an increase in satisfied customers.

1 **Be a "double checker."**

Learn to use those words. Everyone loves it when you double check something for them. Even if you're pretty sure the item is out of stock or the appointment is filled or there is no room available, it sounds so good to hear, "Let me double check that for you."

2 **Pretend it's you.**

If you are working with a customer, either on the phone or in person, and he/she needs something, pretend that it's you. What would *you* want to have happen? What would make *you* happy? What would make *you* satisfied? Here is a great place to remember the Golden Rule: "Do unto others as you would have them do unto you."

3 Get involved.

Let your customers know that you are on their team. If you are ringing up a purchase for someone, mention how nice their choice is. If you're helping someone with a trip of some sort, get excited with them. When customers feel as though you're part of the package, they love it.

4 Stay focused.

Eye contact is critical in delivering excellent customer service. Heads that turn on a spindle and look everywhere but at the customer get very few good marks in customer service. Eye contact shows that you are listening. If you're on the phone, eye contact is definitely difficult. We can, however, learn to stay focused on the phone. Don't type unless it pertains to what you are doing. Don't read something while you're on the phone. *Stay focused* on the caller, even without eye contact.

5 Do something extra.

There's usually always *something* you can do for the customer that's extra. In most cases, it won't even cost very much. For example, keep a stock of penny lollipops—or balloons or coloring books and crayons—for kids when they come into your store with their parents. Spend a few dollars if you have the budgets for those "giveaways." Nail clippers, key chains, mouse pads—customers *love* that something extra, oddly enough, even if they can't use it. The thought of getting something *free* is very special to the customer.

6 Show your teeth.

(In Telephone Doctor language, that means *smile*.) There are many people who think they're smiling, but aren't. So the Telephone Doctor's motto is: **show your teeth.** Smiling is one of the best customer service techniques there is. It's so frustrating to walk into a store, or call someplace, and not see or hear a smile. (And yes, you *can* hear a smile!)

7 Ask questions.

A super way to offer superior customer service is to *ask questions.* Build on what the customer is talking about. Listen for one or two words that you can ask something about. Even a simple "Tell me more" will work. Once the customer is talking, you will be able to help them much better.

8 Use complete sentences.

One-word answers are semi-useless in customer service. And one-word answers are definitely perceived as rude. "Yes," "no," and the like, tell the customer "I'm not really interested in you or what you need."

9 Care.

Most people have what the Telephone Doctor calls the *care gene.* Some of us use it more than others. We just forget we have it. Learn to *care* about your customers' needs. *Care* what they are referring to. *Care* about your customers and they will take care of you.

10 Laugh at appropriate times.

Laughter will lighten the load. Everyone likes to laugh, some even in the darkest moments. Take the time to laugh and enjoy your customers.

Put any one of these Telephone Doctor customer service tips into action and watch what happens. They intertwine with each other and make customer service special. Use all 10, and expect more business.

Take *care* of your customers and they'll take *care* of you.

10 Things Your Customers Won't Tell You, But We Will

Most business owners know that customers will walk—take their business elsewhere if they're not treated as they'd like to be. But how does a business owner find out what the customer really likes or dislikes?

Well, as the Telephone Doctor, we have learned from your customers what they won't tell you. Here are 10 things only your best friend will tell you (by the way, that would be us...the Telephone Doctor.)

1 "Nobody greeted me when I walked into your store. No one said, 'Hello,' no one asked if they could help me, and no one said goodbye when I walked out. Well, at least I wasn't any trouble."

2 "Your sales staff looked tired. Yea, they did. Otherwise why wouldn't they greet me with a big smile and some enthusiasm? It didn't look like they even wanted me in the place."

3 "I bought a lot of stuff. I couldn't believe no one said, 'Thank you.' No one told me to enjoy my purchase. I did get a lukewarm 'Have a nice day.' But it was said so routinely, it didn't mean anything to me."

4 "When I phoned for some information, my call was treated as an annoyance. I sensed very little desire to be of any real help. Do you know what I did then? I called a few more places until I found one that sounded as though they wanted my order."

5 "Whoever answered your phone never identified themselves. I happen to like to know who I'm talking with and when I don't, it hurts any trust I might give your company."

6 "During the phone call, the voice of whoever answered sounded aggressive and challenging. I didn't feel very welcomed."

7 "When I walked in, all your employees were talking and laughing amongst themselves and ignored me until I asked a question."

8 "There was no management around. Remember the old saying 'when the boss is away, the mice will play?' Guess what? They do!"

9 "When I told your staff about my problem, which was important to me, no one sympathized with me. It was 'business as usual' for them."

10 "Everyone looked angry. No one was smiling. Remember, sometimes it's the things you 'don't do' that make me want to go elsewhere."

> ## What else won't your customers tell you?

Are You Guilty?

What's your definition of customer service? What unprofessional behavior irritates you the most when, as a consumer, you are interacting with a company?

Sometimes, customer service that is perceived as rude is not intentional and often is the result of absent-mindedness or carelessness on behalf of an employee. Either way, bad customer service can translate into lower sales and lost business.

Based on the Telephone Doctor surveys, we've compiled 15 customer service NO NOs. They are listed below, along with Telephone Doctor's guidelines (in parentheses) on how to do it right. Believe me, there are plenty more, but these are at the top of the list.

If your company's customer service managers and front-line employees are guilty of any of these, it's time for some action. Otherwise, you may have an image problem that could sabotage your effort to produce and market great products.

1. Your employees are having a bad day and their foul mood carries over in conversations with customers. (Everyone has bad days, but customer service employees need to keep theirs to themselves.)

2. Your employees hang up on angry customers. (Iron-clad rule: *Never* hang up on anyone. When we hang up, we label ourselves as rude.)

3. Phone calls or voicemail messages aren't returned, even when customers leave their phone numbers. (Call customers back as soon as you can, or have calls returned on your behalf.)

4. Your employees put callers on hold without asking them first, as a courtesy. (Ask customers politely if you can put them on hold; very few will complain or say "No way!")

5. Your employees put callers on a speakerphone without asking them first if it's OK. (It's courteous to ask customers if they mind being on speaker phone.)

6. Your employees eat, drink, or chew gum while talking with customers on the phone or face-to-face. (A telephone mouthpiece is like a microphone; noises can easily be picked up. Employees need to eat their meals away from the phone and away from customers, and should save that stick of gum for break time.)

7. You have call waiting on your business lines and your employees frequently interrupt existing calls to take new calls. (One interruption in a call might be excusable; beyond that, you are crossing the "rude" threshold. Do your best to be prepared with enough staff for peak calling times.)

8. Your employees refuse or forget to use the words "please," "thank you," and "you're welcome." (Please use these words generously, thank you.)

9. Your employees hold side conversations with friends or each other while talking to customers. Or they make personal calls on cell phones. (Don't do either of these.)

10. Your employees seem incapable of offering more than one-word answers. (One-word answers come across as rude and uncaring.)

11. Your employees do provide more than one-word answers, but a lot of the words are grounded in company or industry jargon that many customers don't understand. (If you sell tech products, for example, don't casually drop in abbreviations such as APIs, ISVs, SMTP, or TCP/IP.)

12. Your employees request that customers call them back when the employees aren't so busy. (Customers should never be told to call back. Request the customer's number instead.)

13. Your employees rush customers, forcing them off the phone or out the door at the earliest opportunity. (Rushing threatens customers—take your time.)

14. Your employees obnoxiously bellow, "What's this in reference to?" effectively humbling customers and belittling their requests. (Screening techniques can be used with a little more warmth and finesse. If a caller has mistakenly come your way, do your best to point him or her in the right direction.)

15. Your employees freely admit to customers that they hate their jobs. (This simply makes the entire company look bad. And don't think such a moment of candor or lapse in judgment won't get back to the boss.)

In defense of customer service workers, customers can be rude too. And customer service jobs can often be thankless, with little motivation or incentive to do the job right.

But the problem here is that life for customer service employees may not be fair. Customers can be rude and get away with it. Employees cannot—if they want to help their companies succeed and keep their jobs as well.

Don't let your customers *vent* about you.

Art of Apologizing:
A Short Course

Gee, I'm so sorry
Sorry 'bout that
My apologies, I didn't mean to...

There are probably dozens of ways to apologize and many more ways of accepting one.

How important is an apology?

Why do we apologize?

And what words seem to work better than others?

You get the picture.

When you look up the word *apology*, it reads:

To express or make an apology; acknowledging
failings or faults

And the words *I'm sorry* and *I apologize* are *not* always interchangeable. For example, a friend's parent passes away and we typically say, "I'm so sorry to hear about your loss." "I apologize your father passed away" just doesn't seem right.

However, both can be easily used in an apology—to acknowledge a failing or fault.

When you accidentally bump into someone at the mall, instinctively you would most likely say, "Oh, I'm so sorry," or you could say, "I apologize, I wasn't watching where I was going." In this case, they're interchangeable. Think for a moment, though, what you're thinking when someone bumps into you and they don't apologize? Hmmmm?

On a recent bumpy flight, the pilot came on and said, "I apologize for the bumpy flight." He also could have said, "Sorry folks, for the bumpy flight." Again, interchangeable.

Apologies in Business vs. Personal

It seems as though personal apologies may be a little easier to make than a business apology. In my opinion, that's because we normally know the person fairly well in the personal setting and can figure out what to say and do a little easier. And often we can even send candy, flowers, or something else in a bribery fashion so to speak.

However, when something happens in a business setting and the customer is irate and in need of an apology, that's a different story. In many cases, we don't get to meet all of our customers, and if we do, it's normally on a pretty limited basis. Most of the time, it's a phone call. And then, of course, even if we are more familiar with the business customer, where is that line in the sand? Dare we cross over it?

For an apology in the business arena, we suggest using the word *apologize*. It's a classier word—it raises the bar. To just be "sorry" for something can easily diminish the effectiveness of the apology:

"Mr. Smith, I apologize for sending the wrong invoice. That's got to be very frustrating."

To simply push it away with, "Sorry about sending the wrong invoice" takes the sensitivity and meaningfulness away.

And what if you're *not* wrong and the customer still perceives you as wrong? Do you still need to apologize? Of course you do. It doesn't matter if you're right or wrong. When the customer perceives you're wrong, you're wrong.

And for those who say "the customer is always right," we ask you to change that to the mentality we use: "the customer always thinks they're right." And that's the perception we need to deal with.

Timing of Apology

The immediacy of an apology is key. Whichever you use, "I'm sorry" or "I apologize," do not delay. The sooner those words are used, the closer they are to the happening, the more effective they are.

Don't wait to say I'm sorry or I apologize. They're like please and thank you. Important and very relevant.

Easy Rule of Thumb on When to Use Which Word

You're *sorry* when you step on someone's toes (a human emotion).

We *apologize* when the customer is unhappy. He perceives we have done something wrong; we failed (an incident).

Ineffective Apologies

You hear it all the time: "Sorry 'bout that." That's a cliché, not an apology, lose it.

You should always offer a complete apology: "I'm sorry I gave you the wrong change." "Sorry 'bout that" doesn't cut it.

Apologies *do* work.

Back on Track

What do you do with a customer, client, etc., who wants to talk forever when you have a deadline to meet and really cannot afford to spend time on the phone or in a meeting with them?

How do we handle it? Let's say you're on a deadline or in the middle of a very, very important project. Ring, ring. You pick up the phone with your normal nice greeting, "Good morning. Customer Service Department. This is Mary." And out blasts someone who has absolutely nothing to do today. "Hi, Mary," they yell happily at you. "Guess who I saw last night at the movie?" With your deadline looming, you really don't have time to play games now, do you? Or suppose you are finished talking business and the caller now wants to stay on the line and "play." Wow, can that be frustrating!

Since it's the customer service rep's job to constantly be in control of a phone call, you need the exact words to say, and telling someone you're on a deadline or in a rush doesn't cut it. First of all, if they're not a working person, they cannot identify with a deadline. And even if they are in business themselves, they usually don't consider your deadline as important as theirs. I wish it wasn't true, but it happens to me a lot too.

The Telephone Doctor's "back on track" technique allows you to stay in control. Let's say your caller is "wandering," to put it nicely. Simply put that great big smile on your face and tell the caller, "I would love to hear about your great grandmother's train ride across the country; however, I know you called about something for your "X" and I want to be able to help you. Now, what was it you needed?" You're right back on track.

The back on track technique is for the "wanderer." The other way to end a conversation gracefully is when you've concluded the business portion of the call and the caller wants to "play." Simply tell them, "I would love to hear about the movie you saw last night. I heard it was great; however, I need to get off the phone and finish my project by 3:00 p.m. And I know you understand. Thanks so much for calling and have a great day." Or you can tell the caller that you'd love to hear about the movie they saw last night by saying, "Let me have a number where I can call you back. I need to finish a project by 3:00 today."

Once you get the back on track technique down pat, you'll wonder how you ever got hooked into those types of calls.

It's your job to keep the customer on track!

Booth Customer Service 101

Anyone who has ever worked a booth at a tradeshow knows it's just that—*work*. It's lots of work, and sometimes, there's no time for lunch. It often entails long hours, and the long hours are sometimes not very busy. And believe it or not, not being very busy can make you more tired than when you are busy.

Bottom line, put all those items together and sometimes we forget our customer service manners at a booth.

There are lots of articles on boothmanship. This one is on service. Here are the Telephone Doctor's top five tips on *great* booth service. The Telephone Doctor has won several boothmanship awards by adhering to these tips, so we know they work.

1 **Make eye contact.**

This is a face-to-face situation. Eye contact is a must. Looking around the area trying to see who else is there isn't good customer service to the person in front of you. Lock eyes with your prospect and give him/her your complete attention.

2 **Extend your hand.**

Way too many booth folks don't do this. Think of it as that in-person store or office visit. Shake hands. Offer yours first. And don't forget, they have a badge, so use their name!

3 Don't sit down at your booth—*ever!*

This one is difficult, but important. We at Telephone Doctor have a big customer service rule—*no one* sits down unless you're with a client. *No one.* If you feel you must sit down, leave the booth. Go somewhere else to sit. Sitting down at the booth gives off bad vibes.

4 Be considerate.

People visiting your booth get a ton of stuff at the trade show they don't want. They take it just so they don't hurt your feelings. (Trust me, at the first opportunity, it's all pitched.) Ask the client or the prospect, "You have so much already to schlep around...may I mail our product/service information to you?" Then get their business card and make a note "client requests information be sent."

Then, when you get back to the office, you have what is known as a "warm" lead. You can call that client, or prospect, and remind him/her that you met at the show, he/she stopped at the booth, and you promised to send something; is this a good time to receive it? This particular "customer survival tip" is most appreciated. It says that you understand that they have a lot to carry home, and you appreciate their time.

5 Smile.

It hurts me to write this one, but when I go through a tradeshow where we're exhibiting (or not), I watch the other booths and it's sad to see how many folks aren't smiling. So last, but not least, use our Telephone

Doctor **cardinal rule: A phony smile is better than a real frown.** If I took pictures of folks manning the booths and showed them how sad/bad they looked, they wouldn't be too happy. Why wait till a customer comes to the booth to smile? Don't forget another Telephone Doctor rule is **smile *before* you know who it is.**

There are hundreds of other booth customer service tips, but getting these five down pat are instrumental in making your booth more productive and giving *better* booth customer service to all your prospects.

Good luck and have fun. After all, that's what it's all about.

**Boothmanship is an art...
not a science.**

Candy Store Story

A while back, we were on vacation in the outskirts of beautiful Seattle. That would be 11 of us. (It's more of a trip, though, instead of vacation, if you know what I mean.)

After a great dinner, we went for a walk in the small town of Snoqualmie. It was near 8:00 p.m. and, as they say, "they rolled up the sidewalks." Nothing was open. It was still light out so we walked and browsed through the town.

We passed a candy store, which also had ice cream. We all got excited and wanted to get some candy and ice cream (we hadn't yet had dessert).

"Oh, too bad," said one of the folks in the group. "It's closed." The big red OPEN sign now blinked CLOSED.

We pushed on the door anyway and even though it didn't move, we didn't want to believe it was closed. Of course it was.

The kids were upset. Each had their own words for the closed candy store. The adults shrugged and felt "oh, too bad, sure would have been good."

One person in our group said, "Oh, there's someone in the back of the store. But he's not looking out here." The group walked on.

As the others in our group walked on, I stopped, knocked on the door and waited. The man inside waved, but he didn't move to the door to open it.

I knocked again (louder). He waved again. I waved back, but this time I yelled, "We're from St. Louis and never had any Salish candy. There are 11 of us and we're hungry!"

The man walked over to the door and opened it. I explained a little more how this was our first trip to the area, we didn't get dessert at the restaurant, and we'd love to buy a lot of candy. He looked to his partner, shrugged his shoulders and said in a warm friendly voice, "Well, come on in."

To make a long story short, after $65 worth of candy and ice cream, we were all happy campers, including the owner I'm sure.

A couple of lessons here:

#1. Obviously a smart owner. The store was closed; he heard the plea of customers on vacation, and was kind enough to open the door. All to his credit and benefit!

#2. Just because a sign says CLOSED doesn't always mean it is!

Passive: The passive individual saw the closed sign and thought, "Gee, I missed out" and moved on.

Average: The average person wished it were open and thought, "Oh, maybe we'll get back."

Proactive: The proactive person didn't believe the store was closed.

What would you have done?

After you open the candy store, go in for the chocolate.

Can You Tell I'm Smiling?

There's rarely a program I present that someone doesn't ask me if smiling is really that important, either on the phone or in person. People actually ask me: "Nancy, can you really hear a smile?" Yes, Virginia, you can really hear a smile. And your caller can hear the lack of a smile as well.

So this is an article about *smiling* and the reasons for it. Now, if you happen to already be a smiler, you might want to pass this article on to someone who isn't or doesn't know that you *can hear* a smile.

First, let's see the word *smile* from *Webster's Dictionary:*

smile: To smile, be astonished; to have or take on a facial expression, showing pleasure, amusement, affection, friendliness, irony, etc.... and characterized by an upward curving of the corners of the mouth and a sparking of the eyes

See! It's something most everyone can easily do.

And if it's that easy, don't you wonder why more people don't do it? Have you ever been in a store or just been walking around, and see that people aren't smiling. Even when you start talking with them?

A recent *New York Times* review by Roxana Popescu of the book *A Brief History of the Smile* written by Angus Trumble asks a very good question: "Why do English speaking people say 'cheese' to make you smile, but Chinese speakers say 'eggplant'?" And Trumble continues, "The spontaneous smile of the little child is essentially truthful."

Certainly we all know not saying "please" and "thank you" is usually considered rude, but the list of rude behavior is much longer than those offenses. I'm not sure why we constantly need to be reminded to smile, but we do. You'd think it was common sense to smile when you're with a customer on the phone or in person. Ah, but common sense is not that common now, is it?

Will a smile help? As my mother used to say, "It couldn't hurt." We suggest keeping a mirror by your desk. Having a mirror is a good reminder to keep a smile on your face when you're talking with customers.

A phony smile is better than a real frown.

Company Welcome Mat

Customers should be treated as welcome guests when they call an organization; instead, they're often treated like an interruption or, even worse, an annoyance. More than 90 percent of all customer service includes a telephone call. That said, customer service mistakes happen any time and in many ways, whichever way you communicate with your customers.

These customer service tips will help you start or benchmark your own customer service training program. Bring your staff together at a time when everyone can attend and talk about any frustrating customer events. Discuss how they handled them versus how it could have been done. The meeting can be short, maybe 15 minutes, and it doesn't need to be daily—but it does need to be done. Not having a customer service training program in place can cost every organization revenue and customers. Poor customer service creates a negative image for the entire organization, no matter how wonderful the products or services are that you offer.

And if staff have the attitude that there's no competitive organization for customers to go to, tell them that may be right, but if one customer tells another about a negative experience and so on down the line, more customers will leave your business. Then staff jobs will be lost, and eventually, bang—no organization at all.

Here are three of the biggest service mistakes that are most likely to anger customers into lifelong resentment toward an organization:

MISTAKE 1: NOT SMILING

Solution: Smile. It sounds insanely simplistic, doesn't it? We're taught early that a smile can get us a lot. This is true even as adults, especially on the telephone. Since the telephone is the most commonly used mode of communication, we need to understand why a smile works—because you can hear a smile over the phone. We recommend keeping a mirror by your desk, so when you pick up the receiver, you can tell if you're smiling.

OK, OK, sometimes we don't feel like smiling. Well do you know what? Smile anyway. The customer doesn't care if you feel like smiling or not. At the Telephone Doctor, smiling before you pick up the phone is a condition of employment; not smiling is grounds for termination, and, yes, I have exercised that option. With customer service as our top priority, we simply don't tolerate not smiling before you pick up the phone. Frankly, I'd rather have the customer think your office is closed than to have you answer the phone in a negative mood. (*Yes,* the caller *can hear* the smile.)

MISTAKE 2: NOT ACKNOWLEDGING A CUSTOMER'S REQUEST OR PROBLEM

Solution: Rapid responses: we have a "mental stamp" at the Telephone Doctor that reads "RR," which means, "This request or piece of information needs an immediate and rapid response." Requests and problems need to be handled sooner rather than later. Delaying a request can cause more problems than the original request.

Another good habit to get into is to ask the customer: "By the way, when will you need this, Mr. Jones?" The Telephone Doctor surveys found that when a customer is asked when he or she would like to receive the needed information,

80 percent did not automatically respond, "I need it now," as you might expect. Thus, you don't have to promise, "I'll get that to you right away." Often, customers won't need something until tomorrow or next week. Asking for a time-table is good customer service.

And, by the way, "as soon as possible" is not a time. Confirm a date or time.

MISTAKE 3: IMMEDIATELY REJECTING A REQUEST

Solution: Be a "double-checker." It's so easy to tell people, "We don't have it," or "Sorry, it's past the deadline," or "We ran out of that report." Instead, try a soft rejection: "The last time I checked it wasn't available, but let me double-check on that for you." It's a wonderful way to defuse any disappointment about you not having what the customer called for in the first place. This simple statement immedi-ately defuses some of the tension of not being able to fulfill a request completely. And often when we do double-check, we find a way to get what the person wanted after all.

You now have three techniques (simple that they are) to kick start or benchmark your customer service training pro-gram. To make these techniques happen, the entire staff—from president to maintenance—needs to embrace the customer service program or it won't work. Be firm. The organization's entire image is at stake since it is unlikely to get a second chance.

Don't have time? Make time. What or who is more impor-tant than those customers? You'll be surprised at how much fun it is to hear a customer say, "Thanks, you've been super."

 Mistakes aren't fun for anyone.

Emotional Leakage
(Getting Mad at Peter and Taking it Out on Paul)

We've all seen it happen: a coworker comes into work storming angry; has his mouth turned down in a frown; walks through the office without saying hello to anyone; sits down at his desk and starts barking orders to his coworkers; doesn't come out of his office; and when his phone rings, picks it up and bellows out "Yea?" Sad isn't it? Something must have happened before he got to work, and he carried it right inside the building. The Telephone Doctor calls this "emotional leakage," and we cure it all the time.

Hey, it's no fun to get up on the wrong side of the bed in the morning. And it's sure not fun to get a flat tire on the way to work or to argue with someone before breakfast. It's unfortunate that some people aren't able to shake it off and move on about their business.

Emotional leakage is getting mad at Peter and taking it out on Paul. Not right, not fair, not fun. Taking a negative emotion out on someone who wasn't involved—how rude can you get?

If emotionally leaking on coworkers isn't fair, then emotionally leaking on customers is even worse than not fair. The customer or coworker, in most cases, wasn't involved with whatever put you in a bad mood, so why take it out on them? Few things are more unfair and damaging to a relationship than emotional leaking a negative experience on someone who wasn't involved. And yet, unfortunately, it happens every day—at home, in the office, on the streets, in stores.

While shopping the other day, the person helping me was obviously not in a good mood at all. In fact, I think if she smiled, her face would have cracked. She gave me one-word answers and kept turning her head to see who was coming or going. (I wasn't sure.) Normally, I walk out on that type of service. It's just not worth my time to be treated like that. But this time, I was in a hurry and needed the product. So I did something I don't normally do...I asked her if everything was all right? Was she OK? I tried to make it sound as though I was interested (even though I wasn't), but I sure didn't want her negative emotions leaking on me any longer.

With a big sigh, and a sad face, she told me she and her boyfriend had a big fight the night before and she was hoping he'd come by and apologize. "Excuse me," I said, "was I with you?" Believe it or not she smiled and said, "Of course not." Then I nicely told her, "If I wasn't there, I don't want to be part of that argument."

She started to apologize, as well she should. Then I thought about a vase I had once. I dropped it. It broke into several pieces. My husband Dick and I talked about whether we should take it somewhere and have a professional put it back together. Dick said, "We can do that if you'd like, but it will never be the same. You'll always feel the cracks."

And so it is with our coworkers and customers. You can be in a bad mood—be it an argument, a flat tire, or breaking your favorite item, and you can apologize, but people still remember how you treated them and how you made them feel. And remember they will—for a long time, too.

So how do we cure emotional leakage? It's a quick four-step process:

1. Stop what you're doing.

2. Take a deep breath.

3. Put on a phony smile (yes, you can).

4. Regain your professional composure. And then talk with the person—in person or on the phone.

Emotionally leaking on someone is *never* right.

There are times others emotionally leak on us. Think how you feel when that happens to you, and then remember to never emotionally leak on others.

**It's not the other person's fault!
Don't take it out on them.**

How to Deliver Bad News

"Your order is ready."
"I'm glad all went well."
"Your items came in early."
"This is to confirm your appointment."
"I'm happy to say the rates will remain the same."

These are all easy to say when things go well. But what happens when things don't go your way and we need to let the customer know that? Not so easy is it? Well it can be, if you know how to deliver bad news.

The first thing you need to do is don't **over promise.** Guaranteeing a delivery date or price can be dangerous, especially if it's not in writing. And delays happen. Things happen that are totally out of our control, making shipments late and causing appointments to be cancelled.

One of the best examples of this is when you're pregnant and make an appointment with your doctor. It's safe to say that any woman who's been through this will have heard these words sometime during the nine months: "Sorry, Mrs. Smith, the Doctor had to be at the hospital for a delivery so we'll need to reschedule your appointment." This, after you've hurried to make your appointment on time.

And I'm betting we've all heard this one: "Your meal should be here in just a few minutes" (after a rather lengthy wait).

So what's the best way to deliver bad news?

There's a great saying about "under promise and over deliver." That's one way to exceed customer expectations. It's when we over promise and under deliver that causes problems—making promises on shipments or other things we cannot control.

So wouldn't it make sense for the doctor's receptionist to say something like this at the time of the appointment: "Mrs. Smith, this will confirm your appointment on Tuesday at 2:00 p.m., July 1st; however, it'll be a good idea to give us a call 30 to 45 minutes ahead of time so we can let you know if the doctor was called in for a delivery to save you a trip." In other words, handle the objection ahead of time.

The same thing goes with the meal in the restaurant. It would be great if the waiter would say, "I wanted to let you know the meal you just ordered takes about 45 minutes to prepare so you're not looking for it in 15 minutes." Or he might even ask the customers if they're in a hurry, as some of the orders take longer than normal. If you are in a hurry, then you would ask for something that doesn't take so long.

In most cases, it's all about handling the objection ahead of time. In some cases, however, that isn't possible. Let's take a look at some other areas.

Please remember, when possible, never leave bad news on voicemail.

Picture this: You take Fluffy, your dog, into the vet at 9:00 a.m. on the way to work. He had a minor problem over the weekend.

You get to work, go to lunch, come back, listen to your voicemail and hear: "Mrs. Smith? Remember Fluffy? Well I hope you have a good picture of him. He's really, really sick and I'm not sure how long he has. I'm sorry. Thanks for choosing Go Go Vets."

OK, I'm exaggerating. But either way, we wouldn't want to get bad news about certain things on voicemail. That voicemail could have said something like, "Mrs. Smith, this is Go Go Vets and I have a concern about Fluffy that I'd like to discuss with you. When you have time this afternoon, please give us a call at 1-800-WE-DO-DOGS. Thanks so much."

Well, that's better than the first one. Now, let's get a little more realistic and talk about shipment delays and costs of goods that might necessitate a price increase. How do we deliver those things?

On shipment delays, we go back to handling the objection beforehand. In other words, if you're promising a client a certain delivery date or time, be sure you can honor that.

If you can, you might even build in some "fluff" time in the need by date. Example: If the customer needs something by August 1, be honest with him and let him know ahead of time if that's a realistic date for you to deliver. There's very little value to confirming an order you know won't make it in time.

If you can, see if you can put in some extra time where you ask your vendor to have it to you by July 20th so there's 10 days to play with there.

Meeting customer's deadlines is very, very important to them. If you're not able to meet their deadlines, chances are they'll look for someone who can—and will.

So do everything you can to make it happen. Most important, if you do find out an order will be late, give your customer as much advance notice as possible and be prepared to do something extra. Most companies can do something—be it delayed billing, something free, or an extra widget—something to take care of the inconvenience.

What not to say: "I'll try my best." These are useless words. Customers expect that. What were you doing before? *Not* trying your best? Instead, say, "I'll find out a date that we can expect your order to be here."

Never on voicemail if you can help it.

How to Deliver "Business Friendly" Customer Service

Of the many experiences we all have each day involving service, only a few may be memorably pleasant. Some may be OK. Some may even be abrasive.

But don't you think customers would be delighted in being treated one way, to have uniformly excellent service in each encounter? Wouldn't it be great to always receive "business friendly" customer service?

The biggest mistake customer service professionals make is not treating customers friendly enough. Somehow the cold, aloof, reserved, overly formal method of handling people has come to be considered "businesslike." But that's not true. It comes across like frostbite. To the customer it can sound curt, bored, and uncaring. It's costing companies billions of dollars in lost opportunities!

"Business friendly," simply put, is the middle ground between being too cold, impersonal, or uncaring, and the other extreme of being too familiar. It involves the following:

1. Treat every customer as unique; don't become desensitized. During a typical day, you probably handle repetitive questions—the same thing over and over. Toward the end of the day, the "lots-of-calls-fatigue" syndrome sets in and your energy level begins to sag. This is when you need to avoid becoming desensitized, sounding bored and uncaring, and being unpleasant to customers. Every customer deserves the same uniform excellence, no matter what time of the day they call.

51

2. Solve the problem; don't argue! When customers are wrong, and sometimes they are, it's not a good idea to tell them that they are wrong. Don't argue. Good "business friendly" customer service focuses on solving the problem, not identifying and placing the blame.

3. Show empathy; don't ignore what the customer says. Empathy is defined as the ability to share in another's emotions, thoughts, or feelings. When someone describes a problem or a situation, don't ignore it. Say something that shows you heard, understand, and share in the matter. Be empathetic. Reach out to involve yourself in the caller's experience. This indicates that you're being "business friendly."

4. Smile; don't be cold! A smile in your voice makes all the difference in the world. Yes, you can hear it! Without the smile in your voice, the listener's perception is that you aren't very friendly. It's like having a friendly expression on your face when you meet someone. Your smile is your friendly facial expression on the telephone.

As a customer service professional, make it your goal to reach out and treat every customer with the same warm and caring manner. Your goal is uniform excellence. Make every contact memorably pleasant. To do that, make the Telephone Doctor "business friendly" your goal.

Take the friendly out of business friendly and all you have is business, business as usual. Not good.

Listen Up!

Do we really *listen?* Do we really *hear* what people are saying? Are there any methods, tricks, ideas, tips, or techniques to make us be better listeners? We at Telephone Doctor believe there are.

Taken from our DVD on listening skills, below are some ideas to help those who are having trouble being good listeners. In truth, some of us aren't good listeners. What do some people do that others don't in order to be a good listener? If you're going to ask great questions, then you need to listen to the answers you're going to get.

Let me ask you: What do you think the difference is between listening and hearing? Don't we all listen? Don't we all hear people talk? First, let's explain the difference. Hearing is physical and listening is mental.

It's pretty simple. Take a TV commercial. We normally hear it, but do we always listen to it? Probably not, especially if it's about something we're not particularly interested in for ourselves or even others.

There were plenty of commercials that I "heard" on TV, but I didn't really listen to them because they didn't interest me. Getting the picture?

Take the Super Bowl ads. We talk about them before they're even on TV. How many can you remember now? My guess is you'll recall those that were of "interest" to you. You listened to them. We all "heard" them. We watched them. But again, how many did we *really* listen to?

OK, heads up. Here are six easy steps to becoming a better listener. There are more, for sure, but starting with these will help you a lot.

1 **Decide to be a better listener.**

That's like an attitude. You can really decide to be a good listener. It's a decision. Will everything be of interest or value to you? Maybe not, but not listening might be dangerous. So make a mental decision to listen better to those you talk with, especially if you have asked them a question and they answer. You need to *listen* to them.

2 **Welcome the customer.**

Welcome the customer on the phone or in person, in business, or at a social event. We need to make the person feel welcomed. That in turn helps make you a much better listener. Be obviously friendly when you're talking with a customer, you've got to be sincere. Most folks can tell when you're not. So bring a welcoming phrase to the table and use it to make the customer feel as though he's a long lost friend.

3 **Concentrate.**

This is not the time for multitasking. And today, we can all turn to the left or right and catch someone texting and probably having an in-person conversation as well. One of these things will be in trouble. We simply cannot do two things well at once. Your concentration must be on the customer, again, in person or on the phone. Do nothing else but *listen.*

4 **Keep an open mind.**

Why do we need to do this? I'll tell you why. There are some of us who think we know what the other person is going to say before they say it, and so we interrupt or interject our comments before the customer can answer. That's not keeping an open mind. That's interrupting. Some of the time we're right and we do know what the person will say. But it's important to put your teeth in your tongue and not interrupt. By keeping an open mind, you'll gain more information as well.

5 Give verbal feedback.

Talking with someone and not acknowledging what they're talking about is very frustrating for him/her; especially on the phone, because we don't even have body language to check out. So a few "I see," "That's good," "OK," "Interesting," and a few words and phrases like that help the person feel as though you're listening and listening well. In person, you have the ability to nod and smile and they can *see* your expressions. However, on the phone, we need verbal feedback. And be careful that you're not saying the same word over and over, such as OK, OK, OK, OK. That's boring to both of you.

6 Take notes as you talk.

And yes, even in person. That's perfectly acceptable. Taking notes and letting the person know you are doing it is a sign of great interest. I do it all the time when I'm on the phone. I tell the client, "I'm taking notes so we can refer to them later and so I don't forget what you're saying." No one has ever said, "Don't do that." Most say, "Good, that's super!" Taking notes so you can refer back is a big compliment. Don't forget to do it.

There you are—six easy steps to becoming a good listener. Enjoy!

Listening is one of the most important skills we can have. Learn to listen.

Passive, Average, or Proactive:

Which are you?

Take the Telephone Doctor's 1-Minute Quiz and Find Out

Read the scenarios below and ask yourself "Which type am I?"

1. The customer says (either on the phone or in person):
    "Tell you what...I've decided not to take the blue widget."
    Answer from a ***passive*** person: "OK, thanks."
    Customer feels nothing.

2. The customer says (either on the phone or in person):
    "Tell you what...I've decided not to take the blue widget."
    Answer from an ***average*** person: "Are you sure?"
    Customer feels slighted.

3. The customer says (either on the phone or in person):
    "Tell you what...I've decided not to take the blue widget."
    Answer from a ***proactive*** person: "Wow! Sorry to hear that. Are you aware there's a widget maker that goes with it at a discounted price? You'll have several uses for it. Why not keep it? You'll love it."
    Customer feels great and buys the widget and the widget maker.

See the difference? Now, which one are you?

Fact: There is nothing wrong with any of these types. We need them all in this busy world. However, we need certain jobs and positions to be proactive.

Passive

The Telephone Doctor's definition is: A passive person receives information and does nothing with it. The dictionary's definition is: Receiving or subjected to an action without responding or initiating an action in return: *the mind viewed as a passive receptacle for sensory experience.* (Our definition is just simpler!)

Passive does not mean a person is bad or shouldn't be helping customers. It simply means they're passive—not active. Are there passive salespeople? Of course there are. The thing about being passive is most people don't like to be called that.

Passive individuals receive information and do nothing with it. It happens all the time. You go into the grocery store and hand the cashier your check (which has *your name* on it). The cashier asks you for identification sometimes. And then does whatever it is they do, hands back your ID, and says, "Thank you." No other words are exchanged. Even though the cashier had your name, it was never used.

This person is passive. Passive individuals receive information and do nothing with it. The cashier had your name: twice—once on the check and once on the ID.

But again, that's not a bad thing. From my experience, those who are in the *passive* mode and put into sales are, in truth, uncomfortable—not bad, just uncomfortable. They're not at ease telling others what is best for them.

So if you have *passive* individuals on your sales team, talk with them; be sure they're happy. Be sure they're comfortable in their job. My bet is they're probably not quite there yet.

Average

It's a fact. It is easier to get an average person to be proactive than it is to get a passive person up to average. It just is.

Let's see what the dictionary says about average: *average, medium, mediocre, fair, middling, indifferent, tolerable.*

Fact: There is a *mass* of average folks out there—millions of them—and I don't want to be one of them. Not sure about you, but I made a decision a long time ago that I didn't want to be average. I didn't want to be in the mass of mediocrity. Again, average folks aren't bad. They're fine upstanding citizens. But they're average, like a lot of people. And they don't stand out to be remembered. If you're in sales, you *want* to be remembered.

Average individuals receive information and honestly try to do something with what they receive. It's just that they don't seem to be able to get over the hurdle. Average folks say a lot of words like "wow" and "gee, that's so interesting." Telephone Doctor calls those "agreement statements" when a person really doesn't know what to say. So you can see an average person is not bad, just not effective.

I'm not sure about you, but the words that define average are nothing I'd like to be called. Yet day after day, millions of people—including salespeople—go about their business being average. And yes, average people make sales. They do. And sometimes they even "fall" into a large order. In truth it's usually not something that they're responsible for doing. The sale just fell into their laps.

59

Average people go about their business being sort of happy with themselves when they could be so much more— sad. I know some average folks I'd love to take under my wing to help them be slightly more proactive.

Proactive

Ah yes, it's the proactive people in this world who *make things happen.* They find the sales. They are detectives. They ask more questions, look a little deeper and always double check to be sure. Very few proactive people take "No" as an acceptable answer (or a final one).

Proactive individuals are exceptional. They are naturally inquisitive. They know it can be done. Proactive people *love* sales. They eat, sleep, and drink *sales.* They love to talk sales, think sales, and do sales. The *sale* is never boring to a proactive person.

Proactive salespeople aren't necessarily workaholics. They enjoy vacations (even relax on them). But back at work, they have the ability to turn "on." Normally upbeat and happy, proactive salespeople seldom wallow in negativity or self pity. They're somehow able to turn that negative into a positive.

Proactive people find a way to get it done. They know "it can be done." They make one more call, research a little more thoroughly, answer one more question, write up one more sale, and never run out of questions to ask.

Proactive people think for their clients. They have solutions. They enjoy solving problems for their clients. They enjoy success. So again I ask, "Which one are you?"

Below being passive is semi-useless.

Personal Accountability

When I ask an audience if they could make, or *ask,* their employees to have *one* trait, one characteristic, one thing that would improve the organization, what would it be? One hundred percent of the time it's *ownership. Responsibility.* That's the winner every time.

I got to thinking of how many times we accuse, blame, and complain when things happen. And I believe they're right. Taking ownership of a situation, event, or problem is rare. We need to stop accusing, blaming, and complaining.

Let's go over the ABC's of personal accountability.

Accusing

Ah, that's so easy, isn't it? *Bob* did it, not me. For example, let's take a simple, nonthreatening situation—an everyday happening versus a customer situation. Let's say my stapler is missing off my desk. How many of us will say, "Who took my stapler?" How many of us accuse rather than say, "Anyone know where I might have put my stapler?"

Big difference. One is accusing and one is taking ownership.

Blaming

Again, let's keep it simple. If you have kids, you know what this is all about. And while accusing and blaming sound similar, they're not. Blaming can be items vs. people. Example: "Wow, I'm gonna be late because of the snow that's supposed to be heading our way." Or we might have said, "Guess I should leave much earlier tomorrow morning; the snow will make for bad traffic and I don't want to be late."

61

See the difference? We blame things as well as people. We blame weather, we blame objects. Those items aren't even able to defend themselves. Stop being a blamer, and take some ownership.

Complaining

Wow. Don't you hear this a lot? "Hi! Gee, it's so hot today." Well ya know what? It's July in New Orleans. Or St. Louis. Or Miami. It gets hot in the summer. And FYI, it gets cold in the winter if you live in cold-weather country.

And I love it when folks complain about a headache. And I ask them if they've taken anything for it to reduce the discomfort. "Nope." Then why complain? *Doing something* proactive easily fixes most complaining!

Stop accusing, blaming, and complaining!

It IS your job. Take the responsibility.

Question: Why is "No Problem" a Big Problem?

We hear what bugs people a lot—and often. Our customers share their random thoughts with us. One of the most common comments recently is when we are told "no problem" instead of a genuine "thank you" or something else that might be more appropriate.

And when a customer is asking for something, it seems the general public would rather hear, "I'll be happy to get that for you" instead of "no problem."

Where did the expression "no problem" come from?

Ever been on a cruise? Well if you have, you know that if you wanted six more desserts, the waiter will tell you "no problem." In fact, everywhere on the ship, people seem to be saying "no problem." The phrase started in the islands and made its way to our country.

Now when you come down to it, it's not a terrible thing to say to someone. And there are many who don't take offense; however, it seems as though there are many more who do! It's not a dirty phrase; there are no swear words. Perhaps though, shall we say, the phrase is inappropriate.

So today we're concentrating on eliminating "no problem" and share a few other phrases that are, shall we say, more "customer friendly;" words that turn people on instead of turning them off.

The other day in a restaurant, I asked for some water without ice. And I got the old "no problem." The person with me said, "Why would getting you water without ice be a problem?" I was used to the expression so I hadn't given it too much thought. However in a recent Friendly Voice newsletter, we received dozens of e-mails offering their thoughts, and "no problem" really bugged them. Hence I listen!

Yes, I thought a more appropriate answer to my request for water with no ice might have been, "Certainly. I will get that for you." Or even mirroring my request like, "Water, no ice? My pleasure."

So when you are tempted to offer up a "no problem," remember that the public would like a genuine and simple "thank you" instead.

Now why is that a problem? LOL!

**Be happy to assist.
Don't be a problem.**

Questions *Are* the Answer

We all ask questions. And when we ask the right way—and the right questions—we can get the best answers.

J. Douglas Edwards, a master sales trainer from years ago, now deceased, made the statement "Questions *are* the Answers." And we so agree with him. To get the right answers, we need to ask the right questions. And there are various types of questioning techniques.

It's like your mother said, "It's not what you say, but how you say it." The Telephone Doctor has defined six questioning techniques to help you get the right answers.

Every salesperson knows that, as Mr. Edwards said, questions *are* the answers. As salespeople, we are taught to ask questions—to talk less and listen more. One of the best ways to listen more is to ask good questions.

From "Do you have the correct time?" to "Where did you go on your vacation?" asking questions can be the key to your success. Let's go over them now. Which type of questioner are you?

Open-Ended Questions

Open-ended questions. These are questions without a fixed limit. They are questions that encourage continued conversation and help you get more information. They're used to get people to open up and talk. Most, but not all, open-ended questions will start with one of these words: *who, what, where, why, when* and *how.* I say *most,* not *all,* because while these are well-known words to ask open-ended questions, they still can get you one-word answers. So while not perfect, open-ended questions will typically get you much more information.

Closed-ended questions. Conversely, closed-ended questions have a fixed limit. They are often answered with a "yes," "no," or a simple statement of fact. Closed-ended questions are usually used to direct the conversation, to get brief, specific information, or to confirm facts.

The next time you watch a movie that has a trial scene, you will see lawyers using open- and closed-ended questions at the right time to get the answers they need or want. Pay attention to how they use them.

Probing questions. Probing questions are used normally after an open-ended question to get yet more information. And that's because sometimes we ask an open-ended question and we only get part of what we need. So it's more of a follow-up to get more information.

Probing questions can start off with "Tell me more about your trip." And probing questions are valuable in getting to the heart of the matter. Oftentimes, you need to offer "aided recall;" something like, "Does the message on the screen say 'Error,' 'Reboot,' or does it just freeze up?" These types of questions are helpful to the customer.

Echo questions. This doesn't mean that you repeat the question 50 times, but it does mean that you take all or part of the statement the customer made, repeat it once, and turn it into a question. For example:

> **Customer:** I didn't get the right information!

> **You:** You didn't get the right information?

> **Customer:** That's correct. I needed all four pages, and I only got two.

See? By using the echo question, the customer gave you "more" information. Good technique!

Leading questions. These are most salespeoples' favorite types of questions. They are often called "tie downs." They are used to cement the information in your favor. They are short phrases used after a statement of fact. They invite agreement and help the customer say "Yes."

For example: "You'll want to see both islands, *won't you?*" or "After 10 years, it's time to get new carpeting, *isn't it?*"

Leading questions are useful in helping someone who's undecided make the right decision.

There is no "last question" in sales.

Retailing Woes Easily Fixed with Seven Simple Customer Service Training Tips

Some companies blame their customer service problems on part-time help. Saying that the part-timers are just that— "part-timers." They don't want to take responsibility. They don't want to take ownership. They just want to take the money and run. They can't wait to get off work.

No matter how your customers come to you, in person or on the phone, ask yourself what type of customer relations training you have. And if there's not one, think again.

"Gee, Nancy, I'm so busy doing other things. There's just no time for this type of training. We're just too busy to stop and train." Too busy to be nice? Too busy to teach your employees customer service? Think again.

It's up to each and every owner or manager to provide some sort of customer service training. Just putting them out there and telling them to, "be nice" or "tell everyone to have a good day," is *not* customer service training.

Whether your customers call you or come into the store, following these Telephone Doctor ground rules can help make your company the one the customer wants to come back to. It *will* give you the competitive edge.

Ground Rule #1: Greet customers first.

Make it a game. If a customer says "Hello" first, you lose. It's amazing how often you can go into a store, any store, walk around, touch things, look at prices, and walk out, all without anyone saying anything to you. The minute a customer walks into the store, the sales staff need to be the ones to say hello first. It's their job to say hello first. It's not the customer's job to do it. That first friendly "Hello" sets the stage—sets the tone to make sure the customer is *in the right place.*

Ground Rule #2: Smile.

Right! It's that simple! Make smiling on-the-job a condition of employment and grounds for termination if staff don't do it. Tell applicants that in the interview process. "We smile here." It's a simple statement and a powerful sales tool. Don't relent on this one—ever! I recently heard about a young man, about 17, who quit his job two weeks after he started. When his folks asked, "Why?" his answer was, "They drove me crazy; they wanted me to smile all the time."

Ground Rule #3: Enthusiasm counts.

Dale Carnegie said it first, and my father said it second. He used to tell me, "Enthusiasm is a disease—let's start an epidemic." And how true that is. When customers bring something to the counter for you to ring up, or even tell you what they want on the phone, get excited. Let them know you care. When customers see, feel, and hear your enthusiasm, you'll ring up a lot more sales. And your enthusiasm is a great setup for up-selling or cross-selling.

Ground Rule #4: Don't point—go show.

How many times have you walked into a store, asked for something, and the salesperson either just nods you to the item or only points to the direction without saying anything. When and if possible, *walk* with customers to the area they need. If that becomes impossible, cheerfully direct them to what they need and give clear, easy, and most important, friendly directions. "Aisle three, on your right" is clear and easy, but not very friendly. This is friendly:

> The new widgets? Sure, we have them. They're great. You'll find them right past the flower section in aisle three. It'll be on your right-hand side right next to the elephant display. (Using landmarks really helps.) Let me know if you're not able to locate them and I'll get someone to help you.

Those are clear, easy, and *friendly* directions. Pointing is plain rude. (Ask *any* waiter to direct you to the restroom and 100% of the time they point. It's possible to give clear directions to that area, too.)

Ground Rule #5: Use *please, thank you,* and *you're welcome.*

Yes, these are still the most favorite words to all customers. I used to be embarrassed to remind attendees to use these words. But I'm easily reminded that it needs to be taught. There's not a three year old who hasn't been told, "Tell the lady thank you, Bobbie. Go on Bobbie, you can say it. Tell her thank you." Some folks don't let the other person go until the child has said, "Thank you." We spend hours teaching our kids those words and then at age 16, what happens?

Ground Rule #6: Pretend it's you.

Ask your staff to make believe it's them walking into the store trying to purchase something. How would they like to be treated? Tell them every customer will go away thinking one of two ways. Either, "Hey those guys were great" or "Hey, I'm never gonna go back there again." And if they think that is not their problem, tell them to think again. If the customers don't come back, you close up and the staff is out of a job. Then it is their problem. Simple.

Ground Rule #7: Make it fun.

It's difficult out there for a lot of folks. Most people want to laugh. It helps make whatever problems they might have a little easier. So if you have the opportunity to have fun on the job, do it! Make their day!

Consider posting this article in an area employees see often. How about a bulletin board? Put this article in their paycheck. Have them read this aloud. They need to know you are serious about customer service. It's *not* just a passing fancy.

These are demanding times. Be extra good to your customers. Have a training program for your staff.

This should be hanging in the back room in every retail store.

R U Rude?

It seems as though everyone has something they consider to be rude. To some, it's something someone says. To others, it's something someone did. Or maybe it's what wasn't said or what wasn't done. It happens all the time.

Nancy's Personal Top 10 Rude List

1. **Not returning a phone call or having it returned on your behalf.** This is the *absolute king of the rudes.* Certainly we all get a lot of calls. (In most cases that's a good thing. Think of what would happen if your phone never rang.) But when someone asks for a return phone call and it's ignored, that is *rude!* OK, OK, there are folks I don't relish talking with, too. But I have the call returned on my behalf and handled that way. If it's someone I don't want to hear from again and rather they stop calling, I can nicely tell them that. Who can blame them for continuing to call when we haven't made our feelings known?

   And if your voicemail message says, "Please leave a message and I'll return your call" and you don't, do you know what that makes you? A big fat fibber! If you're not planning on returning some calls, then leave the part off that says you will return the call. Or tell the truth: "I may or may not return your call!"

2. **Gum chewing on the phone** (or having anything else in your mouth but your tongue at this time). (Oh yeah, chewing gum in a face-to-face sales situation as well.) Social gum chewing is bad enough. Chewing gum or chomping on candy while on a business call is *rude.*

3. **Not sending thank you notes.** When did we stop doing this? Seems as though most folks don't let people know a gift was received. A handwritten thank you note is always appreciated. By the way, form thank you notes are rude as well. If you are going to send a thank you note, jot it down on a note card—handwritten—and mail it. It will be most appreciated. Don't have good handwriting? That's OK; just keep it short. The recipient will see the words *thank you.* (E-mail thank you's are lazy, but at least acceptable.)

4. **Not returning an e-mail.** How easy can that be? Just hit reply and make a comment. Again, I cannot understand ignoring an e-mail. True, e-mail, like voicemail, was not made for entire conversations, but ideal for getting a "yes" or "no" answer or to confirm something one way or the other. At least our e-mail doesn't shout out, "Please e-mail me and I will return your e-mail."

5. **Taking a cell phone call at a social event or restaurant and not removing yourself to a private area.** *No one,* I repeat, *no one,* is interested in your private call. Letting your cell phone ring or taking a call in a business setting is not only rude, but probably will lose the business for you. I love my cell phone. I use it a lot. But when I get a call, I move away from the people I'm with so as not to disturb them.

6. **Bumping into someone or stepping on someone's toes (physically not mentally) and not saying, "Excuse me."** This happens all the time—walking down the street, in a mall, at the airport. I'm amazed at the number of people who don't actually look where they're going. Good thing they're not driving. Bump into me? Please say, "Excuse me" or I'm sorry." Thank you.

7. **Not covering your mouth when you sneeze or cough.**
And a while back, I learned that it's best to sneeze or
cough into your inner elbow instead of using your hand
to cover your mouth. Makes sense to me. I speak at
conferences and people like to come up after I speak
and talk with me. They sneeze, cover their mouth with
their hand, and then nicely offer that hand to me. Yikes!
Yes, I use a lot of hand sanitizer.

8. **Loud voices in an airplane.** To sit behind, in front of, or
across from someone who is shouting to get over the
sound of the airplane motor noise is maddening. It's
rude to shout in those small areas. Same thing goes
when you're in an elevator. I hear people shouting to
the guy who's standing right next to him. It's rude to the
others. FYI. Combining #5 and #8—talking on a cell
phone in an elevator—is *rude!*

9. **Not asking for time to talk when you call someone.**
When you call someone, don't just barge into their lives
as though they've been sitting there waiting for you to
call. I turn down 100 percent of the sales calls I get when
the caller doesn't ask if I have a moment to talk. It's just
a simple little courtesy—and plain old rude if you don't.
Even on a non-sales call to one of your relatives or
friends, it's a nice thing to do. Ask for time to talk. "Do
you have a quick minute, Nancy?" That would work.

10. **Making me wait when there is no one else waiting** and
there are two of you talking to each other. Sorry, but
that happens a lot. That's not just bad customer service.
It's downright *rude.*

OK, those are just some of my *rudes.* Rudes are personal. Remember, in some countries it's a compliment to belch after a meal.

**Everyone gets a little rude
every once in a while.
Check it out.**

Service Mentality

Customer service: Pick up any store ad, and there's probably a line of copy or two about how well you'll be treated when you shop there. Usually the advertisement reads, "We're the best" or "Service is our middle name" or something like that. The phone book advertisements are loaded with commercials for being very customer service minded.

Why then, do we hear so many horror stories about how people were treated? The Telephone Doctor recently surveyed several companies to seek out the traits—the characteristics—of those that have the service mentality. Clearly, not everyone does. The good news is you can learn the skills of the "best." No one has a monopoly on a service mentality.

The Telephone Doctor culled together the seven traits that were among the highest in the survey. Here are the results.

#1. Empathy

This trait won hands down as the most important characteristic when serving customers. In so many cases, you get *apathy,* the exact opposite of *empathy.* Simply put, empathy is putting yourself in the other person's shoes. How would you feel if what happened to them happened to you? True story: On a recent trip, my wallet was stolen. All my credit cards, checkbook, driver's license, and, of course, the few dollars I had in it were gone.

I proceeded to start making the appropriate phone calls to each credit card company—there were four in all. After explaining who I was and that I was at Disneyland and my wallet was stolen with four credit cards, cash, and a checkbook, the person on the other end blurted out, "Name?"

There was no, "Gee, I'm sorry that happened," no "Oh my, how sad." All they wanted was my name. No empathy at all. I hope those people (and by the way, all four credit card companies did the very same thing) never have to go through that loss. All I wanted to hear was a, "Gee, that's so sad," or a plain old, "I'm sorry to hear that,"—someone who understood.

Empathy is the number one ingredient for a service mentality.

#2. Enthusiasm

Ah yes, enthusiasm. Appropriate enthusiasm cannot be replaced. It's a sign of giving service that is above and beyond. When customers feel that you are enthusiastic for them, they just fall right into the palm of your hand. Generating enthusiasm with a customer is perceived as their having made the right decision. It's a confirmation that they've done the right thing. And everyone likes that.

It's the #2 ingredient of a great service mentality. Do you show enough enthusiasm in your job?

#3. Responsibility

Being responsible is so important. Being responsible is living up to a previously agreed commitment. It can be a large responsibility or a small one. Example: I was speaking at a corporate meeting last spring, and when asked by the meeting organizer what my needs were, I told them all I needed was a handheld wireless microphone. "No problem," I was told by the contact. She said she had told "Bob" to have the handheld wireless microphone ready for when I was sup-posed to speak.

Well, when I got to the meeting room, there was only a "lavaliere" microphone—one you clip onto your garment. It wasn't the correct one we ordered, but nonetheless, it would have worked. However, my contact was terribly disappointed. She told me, "You know, I gave Bob the responsibility to get you the handheld and he let me down, which in turn let you down." She continued, "I gave Bob the responsibility of getting you the microphone you needed, and he didn't do it." When you agree to something for a coworker...or a customer...it's key to be responsible and keep your commitment.

#4. Resiliency

How fast can you pop back into a good mood when something has disrupted your schedule? Or do you pout and fret about it, and linger and wallow in it? The ability to bounce back from any adversity is an important service mentality.

We all get hit with some problems during the day— things that weren't what we planned. And as my mother used to tell me, "It's not the problem, Nancy, it's *how* you handle it." As usual, mothers are right. The handling of any situation is what makes the situation good or bad. And if you've been hit with a disappointment or something that you weren't planning on, it's up to you to bounce back—to be resilient. Your customers should never know you were disappointed. Do you need to work late and miss dinner with some friends? Or perhaps you had a minor disagreement with someone. The customer should never know that. Resiliency is needed to have the service mentality.

#5. Balance

Just like the justice scales that need to be kept in balance, so it is with our workload vs. the customer. There's a fine line between pleasing the customer and losing money for the company. In other words, it shouldn't all be one sided. When a customer needs something, that's fine. If, however, we go over the line, it becomes unbalanced and not fair to either the customer or the company.

Finding the right balance at your job and in your company will help you maintain the right balance for both you and the company. Is the customer always right? No... the customer always thinks he's right. We need to know the difference between giving away the store and sticking to company guidelines.

Balance keeps everything in "check."

#6. Ownership

This is my personal favorite because I see it so much as I call and shop around. It runs rampant through the business world. This is the proverbial "it's not my job," or "it's not my department," or "I wasn't here that day," or "I don't know anything about that."

Customers don't care if you were on vacation when something happened and they need help. They don't care if it's not your department. You answered the phone...they're depending on you. You are at the counter to help them now.

If you answered the call, you own the call. Take ownership of the situation. It's not that you'll need to do everything...but taking ownership...and making sure the customer knows that you will find out for them is the key! The Telephone Doctor feels it should never take two people to give good customer service. You get the call. You own the call.

#7. Adaptability

Granted, this service mentality might need some practice, but it is another important ingredient, characteristic, or trait of the service mentality.

Think about the number of people who you help every day, either on the phone or in person. They're all different, aren't they? Not only in culture, color, or accent, but in mood and personality. We need to be able to adapt to all kinds of personalities. Having difficulty understanding someone? Learn to adapt to their particular communication style. Slow talkers? Adapting to them is so important, mostly because slow talkers don't like to be rushed. So rushing a slow talker through a conversation will only make matters worse. You'll need to adapt to those who are slow talkers. And of course, there's the fast talker—who you also need to adapt to. Ask them to please slow down so that you can help them with what they need.

Think of the chameleon, that little lizard-like animal that takes on the color of what it lands on. Chameleons adapt to the color, and usually they're difficult to see. We need to adapt to the situation so that every transaction is a seamless one.

Well, there you have it. The seven traits that make up a service mentality. You probably have some of them. Work on the ones that you don't have or aren't up to par in. Possessing these traits will garner you happier customers (and a happier boss).

Add in some *humor* and some *confidence* to add to the service mentality.

81

Service Recovery: The Art of Damage Control

We all know about customer service. Those of us who are in this industry normally are the ones who genuinely want to help the customer. It's sort of a "high" for us when things go right. But what happens when it all goes wrong? Downhill? How do you recover?

Service recovery is simply the art of damage control, and every industry has damage control. Think about Hollywood. Poor Tom Cruise: he said something bad about Brooke Shields and everyone was out to get him. The PR team went into damage control big time.

And what about when things happen in government? Big time damage control shifts into gear.

And so it must when customer service goes wrong. Think damage control. What can we do over and above in order to gain this customer back? To have them swearing *by* us and not *at* us?

Empowerment

Empowerment is the number one step of service recovery. Each and every employee needs some form of empowerment. They need to know how far they can go to help the customer. Remember our Telephone Doctor rule: It should never take two people to give good customer service.

Any time you escalate a call to a supervisor you are losing ground. The more employees a customer speaks with to get a problem resolved is a step behind the eight ball.

Humor

This will only work when you have a rational customer. And normally when it gets to service recovery, the rationale is lost. However, what we do know is most customers respond in kind to gentle humor.

One of the worse things you can say to a customer is, "I know exactly how you feel." There is simply no way in this world anyone can know how someone else feels. That particular statement will get you in a lot of hot water. Lose it fast. You can say, "I can only imagine how you feel." But best you don't ever walk in the customer's shoes. It won't be a good fit, I promise you.

Service recovery is when you've helped the customer and you can really tell that they're satisfied and that they're back in the groove with your company again. That's true service recovery. When they go from screaming to loving you. And it can be done.

You need a whole lot of empathy or sympathy. You need to listen. You need to care. These are the tools for service recovery. You need to go that "one step beyond." You need to do something the customer is totally not expecting. Something that bowls them over. Each industry has its own bowl over, and sometimes it means taking a loss. But if you're really looking to *save* that customer, you're willing to take that loss, because in the long run, the customer will be so happy and so smitten with your company, they'll be singing your praises to all their friends.

Service recovery is *special.* You see, good customer service is expected. That's nothing new or special. You're supposed to give good customer service. What's the big deal? But often times it all hits the fan and that one customer is just really fired up—mad, bad, screaming, totally out of it. That's when your service recovery needs to kick into gear.

**When the stuff hits the fan,
kick into *recovery mode.***

Spank Them with Your Wallet:

Consumer Confidence Linked Directly to Customer Service

For years, the Telephone Doctor saying has been: "We will pay more for better service." And today, during these challenging times, it means even more.

Fact: There is a direct correlation between consumer confidence and how you treat your customers.

Example: This is a true story: My husband and I were in the St. Louis airport. Some stores had already closed. Vacant areas abounded. We were hungry and there were a few restaurants available to us; none were terribly crowded.

We sat down in a bar and grill—hungry, thirsty, and tired—although not necessarily in that order. It wasn't *that* busy. The waitress finally came after a 10-minute wait. And that was after we got up and asked the hostess if our table came with a waitress (she didn't catch the humor).

Finally! With water and menus, she walks up to the table.

Waitress:	"Take your order?"
Me:	"Yes. Diet Dr. Pepper, please." And as I start to continue, she interrupted.
Waitress:	"We don't have Dr. Pepper."
Me:	"OK, what do you have?"
Waitress:	"Diet Pepsi," she explained.

Me: "OK, then. I'll have a Diet Pepsi", I continued, "and a grilled chicken sandwich please, on whole wheat bread."

Waitress: "We don't have whole wheat bread," she said in the same tone as the Dr. Pepper line.

Me: "OK. Let me double check the menu." Quickly I told her, "How about the burger, no bun, and no chips."

Waitress: "How do you want that cooked?"

Me: "Medium rare, please."

Waitress: (In all seriousness) "We only cook them well done."

Me: (I didn't have the heart to say, "Then why the heck did you ask me how I wanted it cooked?")

Normally, we would laugh our way through this type of situation, but neither Dick, my husband, nor I felt like we wanted to spend any more time or money in this bar and grill, which we have now named "The NO Restaurant." Our eyes locked. We knew exactly what we were going to do. Yes, we went elsewhere.

Spank them with your wallet, we say. It's better retaliation than getting angry and yelling. Since I wrote this article, several other situations have happened to make me spend my money elsewhere. What about you?

No customer service training. I can pretty well guarantee you there had been no customer service training in that bar and grill. No alternatives were suggested. No apologies were made. And we felt as though the waitress was glad to see us leave—one less table to handle.

Everyone thinks they're nice. And we know everyone isn't nice. Some folks, sadly, don't know how to *be nice.* If they did, everyone would be nice. Customer service training is tangible. Explainable. Useful. Understandable. Actionable. "Be nice" is not.

"Be nice" is something your mother might tell you when you're five years old. It's *not* customer service training.

Consumer confidence equals customer service training.
There is a definite correlation between *consumer confidence* and customer service training. No doubt about it. When we feel secure, helped, wanted, needed, and appreciated, that is where we spend our money. Think Nordstrom. Disney. Five-star restaurants. These and many other companies place high value on customer service training.

Fact: When a consumer walks into a location or calls on the phone, they are looking for *confidence* from the person they're talking with at that time. That confidence comes from product and customer service training.

- Increasing *consumer confidence* will help the economy.

- Increasing *consumer confidence* will help businesses both large and small.

- Increasing *consumer confidence* will help the employee.

- Increasing *consumer confidence* is a benefit the business gives the consumer.

What are you doing to increase consumer confidence in your customers?

Five tips for customer service training. Here are five simple, helpful tips based on the Telephone Doctor's Customer Service Training—effective techniques that will increase *consumer confidence* and help this economy.

1 Offer alternatives.

Out of stock? Don't have what the customer needs? Don't let the customer walk. Offer some alternatives. Give them choices. Keep them interested. Don't let them go. It's so easy for the customer just to hang up or walk out and go somewhere else. Give the customer a reason to stay with you.

2 Smile and be friendly.

If there was ever a time to smile and be friendly, it's now. And for those of you who don't feel like smiling, do it anyway! Watch what happens. As for being friendly, that's more than just "can I help you?" It's saying something proactive. Something easy. Something simple. Maybe just a "Good to have you here today" or "Nice to talk with you" or even that great phrase, "Thank you for your business."

3 Be a double checker.

Most salespeople know that "No" is not forever. It gives a whole other meaning to consumer confidence when the customer is told by the salesperson, "The last time I checked we were out of the widgets, but let me double check, just in case I missed them or new ones came in." Double-checking is a great confidence builder! Immediate "No's" are deflators.

4 Ask questions.

We don't need to answer a question as soon as it's asked. We can ask one to gain more information. The more information you have, the easier it becomes to increase consumer confidence. Determine the needs of your customer before trying to "sell" them. Besides, asking questions shows that you are interested and that, in itself, can increase consumer confidence.

5 Do something different.

Did you write a thank you note? Did you call to see how your customer is doing? Did you personally thank them for their business, or for coming to your location, even if there was no purchase?

There is a "mass of gray averages" out there. Those are the people who do nothing to increase consumer confidence. Decide for yourself, and for your business, if you want to be in that mass of gray average or if you'd like to raise the bar and be an "island of excellence in an ocean of mediocrity." The more we can increase consumer confidence, the better off we will be!

> **Customers will go somewhere else when they're not treated right.**

The Telephone Doctor's 6 Cardinal Rules of Customer Service

There are a lot of "rules" in customer service, but few more important than the six we've listed here. Each makes a valid statement and will increase the satisfaction of your customers.

Cardinal Rule #1: *Personal Responsibility/Accountability: Don't Pass the Buck*

One of the most important attributes a company staff member can have is personal responsibility—personal accountability. Those who have it refuse to accuse, blame, and complain. Those who do accuse, blame and complain break one of the most important cardinal rules. "Who" statements accuse and blame. "Who took my stapler?" We should use a more positive manner and take personal responsibility by saying, "I seem to have misplaced my stapler; has anyone seen it?" Remember to take full responsibility with the customer. The customer doesn't like to hear accusing, blaming, and complaining statements. They know when you're passing the buck!

Cardinal Rule #2: *Attend to People before Paperwork*

When a customer walks into your place of business or calls you while you're working on something, Cardinal Rule #2 says drop everything. Attend to that person. Remember, paperwork and other tasks can wait, people should not.

We've all been abused when we go shopping and have been ignored because the salesperson was doing something else. We know how that feels. Let's not abuse our own customers. Remember: People before paperwork.

Cardinal Rule #3: *Don't RUSH Your Customers*

Sure, you may understand something really quickly, but rushing the customer along will only lead to them feeling intimidated. Remember to mirror their speed. Trying to be "done" with a customer as quickly as possible is seen as being rude and uncaring. Rushing threatens customers. Take your time with each and every contact.

Cardinal Rule #4: *Don't Use Company Jargon*

Have you ever gotten a report from a company and not understood it? Some companies have company jargon that makes the CIA wonder what's up. Be very careful not to use your own company jargon on your customers. You and your employees may understand it very well, but the customer may not. And you'll only cause a lot of unnecessary confusion. Spell things out for your customers. Use easy words. Try not to abbreviate. Remember, don't use military language on civilians.

Cardinal Rule #5: *Don't Be Too Busy to Be Nice*

Hey, everyone's busy! That's what it's all about. Being busy does not give you carte blanche to be rude. Remember, you meet the same people going down as you do going up. They'll remember you. And what's worse than being busy? *Not* being busy!

Cardinal Rule #6: *Be Friendly BEFORE You Know Who It Is*

There's a good lesson to be learned here. One Telephone Doctor saying is: Smile BEFORE you know who it is. Often times it's too late. Being friendly before you know who it is will earn you classic customer service points. The customer needs to know you want to work with them, no matter who they are. Remember, sometimes it's way too late to smile and be friendly after you know who it is.

Any one of these tips can boost your customer service!

These represent the *face* of customer service.

Top 10 Customer Service Mistakes

Recently, someone asked about the worst customer service mistakes. So we compiled a list of the ten worst customer service mistakes. Take note and don't let these happen to you!

1 Not being friendly enough.

Without exception, not being friendly is the number one customer service mistake. Customers should be treated as welcomed guests when they call or visit your company. As we've all experienced, sometimes we're treated as an annoyance or an interruption. The Telephone Doctor motto, "Be friendly before you know who it is," is one way to eliminate this mistake.

2 Not maintaining good eye contact.

Heads that twirl on a spindle when you're working with a customer is a big mistake. Keep your eyes on the customer. It's a sure sign that the person you're talking with isn't holding your interest when you're glancing all around. And they'll notice it quickly. Obviously, the Telephone Doctor understands making good eye contact on the phone is a bit difficult, albeit impossible. Therefore, when you're on the phone, you need to be completely focused on the call and the customer. Don't type unless it pertains to the call. Don't read something else; don't do anything but listen to the caller.

3 **Talking with coworkers and ignoring or not acknowledging the customer.**

This customer service mistake unfortunately happens a lot. It seems as though it's more important to continue talking with a coworker than establishing immediate rapport with the customer. Drop the internal conversation as soon as you see the customer. And carrying on a conversation with someone in your office while you're talking with a customer on the phone is a real "no no."

4 **Being rude.**

No one thinks they are rude, certainly not on purpose. However, the customer can perceive many things you do as rude. And as the saying goes, "Perception is reality."

5 **Not being knowledgeable about the product/service.**

When working with a customer, if you're not familiar with the products and services you offer, you'll be making a big mistake. Take the time to learn about your company. Know what's going on. If you are temporary or are new with the company, it's not enough to use that as an excuse. Customers don't care if you're new, if you're working on a temporary assignment, or if it's not your department. All they want is help and information. Ask to be trained. Ask for more information from your company.

Telling customers, "I'm new" or "I'm just a temp" only adds fuel to the fire. You can explain to them that you will find someone to help them as you are "not familiar" with the situation. That at least shows you're going to help them.

6 Leaving customers without telling them where you're going and why.

It's a very good idea to explain to your customers in person or on the phone what you're going to be doing for them. It helps them be more patient. If you need to go "in the back" to get something it's easy to say, "Mr. Jones, the widget you're looking for is in the stock room. Let me go get it for you. I'll be a few moments." The same procedure should apply on the phone. Never tell the caller, "Hold on." Let the caller know where you are going and approximately how long you think you'll be. This will make working with customers easier for both you and them.

7 Blaming others.

It's not the person you blame who will look bad...it's you. Don't blame (or knock) the company, its policy, or any member of the staff. Customers don't want to hear about whose fault it is; they just want the situation fixed. Take full responsibility of the situation at hand.

8 Not double checking.

When customers want something and it's not available, it's how you reject them that's more important than the fact that you are rejecting them. The process of double-checking should become habit forming. It should be a standard operating procedure. It feels so good when you tell someone, "The last time I checked we were out of stock, but let me double check for you to be sure." I personally can think of dozens of times when I asked the person to double check after they told me they were out of things, and what do you know...someone had reordered and the person didn't know about it. It's a big mistake to not double check.

9 **Giving one-word answers.**

We're taught in school that three words make a sentence. Don't answer with one word. Even *yes, no,* and *OK* are perceived as rude and uncaring. A Telephone Doctor reminder: use complete sentences when speaking with your customer.

10 **Head shaking.**

When a customer asks you for something, give them a verbal answer. Shaking your head up and down or back and forth is *not* an appropriate answer. They can't hear your head rattle.

Fixing these customer service mistakes will enhance your ability to work better with customers. Remember, it's the SLDs (subtle little differences) that make the big difference!

> **On the phone or in person,
> not doing these will help a lot.**

What's Your R-T-C Factor?

In interviewing customers around the country, I found that there were several things they value—things a customer wants before the product or service. They boiled down to three basic wants comprising the R-T-C factor: relationship, trust, and consistency. Let's go over them:

R Relationship

Building rapport is an overlooked art. Call many companies and the first word shouted at you is: "Name?" No "nice to meet you by phone" or even a "good morning." There's very little rapport building found in today's customer service. The Telephone Doctor believes the relationship starts within the first 4 to 6 seconds of a phone call or within 45 seconds for an in-person visit. That sets the stage for the rest of the transaction. Plus, it lays the groundwork for possible future business. Rapport building and relationships are vital to every communication exchange.

T Trust

If the customer is unable to trust what you say, the relationship will melt to zero. Gaining the trust of your customer is the *key* to relationship. From following through when you promise to call or fulfilling the company's guarantee statement, creating trust is vital. If those trusts are broken, it's a big fence to mend. Keep your word to gain the trust of your customer. They need to know they can count on you. Before any sale, a customer must buy "you."

C Consistency

The McDonalds hamburger in Cancun, Mexico, tastes the same as the one in Des Moines, Iowa. Why? Consistency. We have learned that the taste will be the same in each of the stores. A business should run with the same consistency. It shouldn't matter who the customer talks with. Personally, I'm skeptical when someone tells me to "Be sure to talk to Joe. He's the best there is." I'd rather hear, "You can talk to anyone in our office."

In summary, the R-T-C factor is what customers look for and deserve in any of their transactions.

> **RTC are great ingredients
> for a successful sale.**

Why I Left the "Dental Implant Guy"

Although this is a story of a dental experience, it could apply to any service provider.

My dentist tells me I need a dental implant. My experience with dental implants is lower than my experience with landing on the moon. So I'm really in his hands. I know that this field relies and depends on referrals. So, of course, I let him refer me to a dental implant guy. It was the implant guy right next to my dentist's office.

I should have realized what I was going to experience when I called to make the appointment.

It wasn't very pleasant. It was cold, impersonal, unfriendly, and unhelpful. And I haven't even gotten to the dental implant guy yet. This was his staff—his ambassadors to the public. "Well," I thought, "this should be interesting."

When I say they were cold and unfriendly, I suppose they wouldn't think that. What I'm talking about is since this was my initial introduction to the office, there should have been some empathy, some interest, and some desire to be sure I was comfortable.

What I wanted to have happen was to have them be interested in me: to ask if this was my first experience with dental implants; to find out if I was apprehensive, scared, nervous; or anything like that.

They made the appointment just as though I was going grocery shopping. This first introduction, this first impression, has never left me. It's embedded in my memory.

OK, then I get to the day of the appointment. This is almost funny, perhaps because of my sense of humor, not because it was humorous. You see, due to my sense of humor, when the unpleasant happens, I tend to find it funny—not joke type funny, but odd type funny.

When I make an appointment by phone and then walk into the office and let them know I'm there and no one acknowledges that they're glad to have me, nice to see me, or any kind of welcome, I find that "odd" funny. Don't you?

"Have a seat, and we'll be right with you" were their welcome words to me. Unfortunately, their "we'll be right with you" and my "we'll be right with you" are miles apart. I don't find 25 minutes "right with you." For the life of me, I can't understand why people don't tell the truth. But then that's a whole other article.

So we get into the chair. Now I'm really scared. But no one seems to care. If they do, I can't tell. They don't ask if I am. The assistant never introduces herself. So I ask her name. I would have felt so much more comfortable if she had said, "Hi Mrs. Friedman, it's nice to meet you. My name is Gail and I'll be Dr. X's assistant with this procedure. We're glad to have you here. I hope this will be a more pleasant experience for you than you might have expected."

Side note: I chose my dentist years ago because when I went to make the appointment, I told the receptionist I have always been very afraid of dentists. She said to me, "Well let me tell you, Dr. F has hands like a butterfly." Man, that sold me. Not only could I visualize the scene, but I know butterflies are soft, gentle, and you aren't even aware when they land on you. And she was right!

But I digress. OK, so now the *implant* guy comes in. I first make sure he will give me the "gas"—no way am I doing this without the gas. I get gas to get my teeth cleaned; I wasn't doing this implant without gas. "Oh yes, we have gas," he says. That's all. And he proceeds to work on me.

Again, no bonding, no rapport building, no conversation. Just start working. It was a cold, unpleasant experience. All his conversation was with "Gail" his assistant. Nothing to me.

What's wrong with this picture? A lot. I can only guess that they don't have patient relations in dental school. I am pretty sure they don't have it in medical school. I just thought dental school would be different.

Well, I had the dental implant done. But I can tell you I would never refer this doctor to anyone. From the appointment to the procedure, it wasn't a great experience.

I trust that the dental folk reading this feel this is a lone instance, but I can tell you from experience and from hearing from others, sadly it's not.

Normally, I jot a few notes at the end of the article as to how to do it right. I'm only hoping that after you read this article and share it with staff that they'll get the picture without needing more information. But just in case they don't get it, here are a few ideas to help you out:

- Welcome the patient (on the phone or in person)

- Smile on the phone and at the patient in person. They like that.

- Assure patients that they are in very good hands.

- Be truthful. If it's going to be 15 minutes, tell patients that. 25 minutes? Tell them that. "Right with you" isn't the truth in so many cases.

- Thank patients for their business.

Since my nature is to look at the sunny/positive side of things, I will tell you that the dental implant guy did follow up a few days later with a phone call to see how I was doing. And while I felt that was a nice gesture, it never erased what happened. Frankly I expect a follow-up call from any one who does surgery on me. That is, in my opinion, a "given."

Dental offices are in customer service too!

Telephone Doctor IQ Quiz

Circle the correct answer.

1. **When on the telephone, "How can I help you?" belongs:**
   A. In the initial greeting.
   B. In the message-taking scenario.
   C. Nowhere. I'm not able to help anyone.

2. **When I'm not able to help a customer on the phone, I should:**
   A. Tell them honestly and thank them for their business and hang up.
   B. Give whatever information I can, right or wrong. Wrong information is better than no information.
   C. Get help immediately and advise the person help is on the way.

3. **When I'm having a bad day, I should:**
   A. Not bother coming into work.
   B. Leave my troubles at the doorstep like the song says.
   C. Tell all my coworkers my troubles to get it off my chest.

4. **Chewing gum at work is:**
   A. OK.
   B. A bad breath refresher.
   C. Downright rude and obnoxious. FAGETABOUTIT!

5. **A mirror at my desk will:**

    A. Keep my ego in check.
    B. Remind me to smile *before* I pick up the phone.
    C. Give me bad luck if it breaks.

6. **Basic customer service skills are important to me because:**

    A. Everyone needs a refresher.
    B. I need a lot of help.
    C. I never learned any.

7. **Internal customer service means:**

    A. Be nice to others who come into my office.
    B. The customer is giving me a stomachache.
    C. Treating my coworkers as customers.

8. **When using voicemail and leaving a message I should:**

    A. Leave my phone number twice and slowly.
    B. Leave a good clean joke to keep them smiling.
    C. Not leave a message; just call back until I reach the caller.

9. **Irate callers/customers are important to our company because:**

    A. It's fun to handle those kinds of calls.
    B. At least we get a second chance to make it right.
    C. I finally get to yell back.

10. **Asking some questions of the customer will:**

    A. Aggravate them.

    B. Show I'm interested in helping.

    C. Be considered being too nosy.

> ## Share this with everyone
> ## in your office.

Telephone Doctor
IQ Quiz Answers

1. Correct answer is B. Anything *after* your name *erases* your name. And on initial greetings, your name is very important. You have answered the phone to help them. It's a given. Those words are best used in a message-taking scenario.

2. Correct answer is C. Be sure you let the customer know that help is on the way. That's the most important part.

3. Correct answer is B. We need to leave our troubles at the door. Arguments with a spouse or a bad hair day is *your* problem. The Telephone Doctor calls that "emotional leakage." That's getting angry at Peter and taking it out on Paul. Not fair, not right, and no fun for the caller.

4. Correct answer is C. No gum at work—ever. End of subject. If you have bad breath—use mouthwash.

5. Correct answer is B. The old Telephone Doctor adage "smile BEFORE you pick up the phone" is the way to make every phone call, or customer contact, a great one. Remember, it's hard to be rude when you're smiling. ☺

6. Correct answer is A. Everyone can use a brush-up course. There's a great saying: "When you're through learning, you're through." Never stop taking those little basic skill lessons you're offered. Even if you do know it all, look how good you'll feel about that!

7. Correct answer is C. We need to treat our coworkers as well as we're going to treat our external customers. Remember: We are customers to each other. We sure don't need any internal conflicts between coworkers and departments.

8. Correct answer is A. Voicemail was meant to take an effective message. Give details and speak conversationally so that the person receiving the message will enjoy and understand the message. Effective messages have concrete information—dates, times, names, situations. Leave your phone number—twice and slowly. Make voicemail work for you, not against you.

9. Correct answer is B. Getting a second chance is golden. And irate callers, while certainly not pleasant, can be the challenge of the day. And they can be satisfied.

10. Correct answer is B. Listening and questioning skills are very important to excellent customer service.

Telephone Doctor 10-Point Customer Service Self-Assessment

Invest three minutes in the health of your organization by completing this 10-Point Customer Service Self-Assessment. To gain greater insights, you're welcome to copy this assessment and distribute it to others in your organization.

   When completing this form, think about your experience, your coworkers' experience, and most important, how you'd imagine your customers might answer each question. Select a number from 1 to 5.

1. Our entire staff has been comprehensively trained on the techniques needed to handle, defuse, and retain angry customers.

     Disagree   1   2   3   4   5   Agree

2. When handling calls from our customers, all our team members employ a uniform, effective greeting.

     Disagree   1   2   3   4   5   Agree

3. When an employee has a performance shortfall, our managers are trained to implement a proven coaching process.

     Disagree   1   2   3   4   5   Agree

4. Customer contact employees at our organization know how to present negative information in a positive way.

     Disagree   1   2   3   4   5   Agree

5. Our team is skilled at knowing how and when to use a variety of questioning techniques in their customer interactions.

>   Disagree   1   2   3   4   5   Agree

6. New employees are well educated on issues such as dress code, limits on personal calls, and steering clear of office politics.

>   Disagree   1   2   3   4   5   Agree

7. Our customer contact employees do a great job of rapport building and making our customers feel like friends.

>   Disagree   1   2   3   4   5   Agree

8. When a team member is having a "bad day," that negative emotion is *never* obvious to a customer.

>   Disagree   1   2   3   4   5   Agree

9. At our organization, coworkers are always treated as well as we try to treat our outside customers.

>   Disagree   1   2   3   4   5   Agree

10. Customers are usually astounded by the high level of care they receive from our team.

>   Disagree   1   2   3   4   5   Agree

Total Score: _____

45–50 – If this is an accurate assessment, we'd like to congratulate you. If your customers rate you this high, you're obviously doing many things very well. We'd like to speak with you about establishing a long-term plan to ensure this level of excellence continues.

27–44 – Most organizations rate themselves in this range, about average, but still not excellent. How would your customers likely answer the same evaluation? We invite you to learn more about our solutions so we can help you close the gap between where you are now and where you should be.

26 or below – Congratulations on recognizing a shortfall. You've taken the first step on the road to improvement. The next critical step is to begin steps to fixing the problem. We look forward to working with you on improving the level of service at your organization www.telephonedoctor.com.

If you have a GAP between where you are and where you need to be in Customer Service, raise the BAR.

21 Great *Unexpected* Customer Service Tips

OK! OK! Yes, there are certainly more than 21 ways to *great* customer service, but rather than overwhelm you, we wanted to start out with a palatable number. And 21 sounded like a good number to me. Any one of these tips will produce better relations in your customer service. The idea is to bring *unexpected great* customer service—things that other folks don't do!

1. Smile! All the time. Right. Don't kid yourself. Just as it can be seen in person, it can be heard on the phone. So as NIKE says, Just Do It!

2. Say something nice at least once a day to someone. I was at the St. Louis airport a while back and the skycap came up to me and said, "Are you going first class or does it just look that way?" That was over 10 years ago and it still seems like yesterday. People remember nice things, just as they remember the not so nice things.

3. Don't ever argue with a customer. You'll lose every single time. Don't even get into the ring with them. "Maybe you're right" is a great saying.

4. If you're sending something to a customer via any method, consider adding a short personal note. Items received without any note or mention of transaction is perceived as cold and rude. A simple "Thank you" on company notepaper will do the trick. It says you stopped to do something special.

5. Use "we" statements when possible rather than "you" statements. *We* is consultative and feels friendlier, and it's far less confrontational.

6. See someone walking into your store/branch/location/ office? Say "hello" loud and clear. Ignoring people, even fellow employees, isn't good customer service.

7. Keep the fences in your organization low. We all know there needs to be rules, guidelines, and policies. However, when there are so many of them, they can make doing business difficult. It's not worth it.

8. Be a double-checker. Often, we can miss something or not know all the details. Most people appreciate hearing, "The last time I checked, we were out of stock on that; however, let me *double check* for you." That particular statement is so comforting. Everyone loves a double-checker.

9. We cannot do two things well at once. If you're working with a customer, on the phone or in person, then focus on that person. Trying to type, or file, or do some paperwork while you're communicating with a customer is dangerous and rude.

10. If your attitude stinks, change it. No one—absolutely no one—wants to be connected with someone with a bad or negative attitude.

11. Respond rapidly. When you receive information from a client, it's a good thing to let them know you *did* receive it and will be working on it. That's good communication.

12. Extend a firm handshake when being introduced to a customer. And *firm* is the key word. That loose, fish-like handshake is not a sign of confidence. *Firm* is key.

118

13. Thank you notes are still thought of as *great.* Take the time to jot several off a day to new, or better yet, long-time clients. E-mailed thank you's are just OK. Unexpected is a personal note.

14. Use your name when you answer the phone. Everyone likes to know who they're talking with.

15. Use your listening skills more often. We all like to talk, mainly to show off how much we know. But listening to what the customer knows is much better. Let others have the stage.

16. It shouldn't take two people to give good customer service. Learn how to handle the situation yourself rather than trying to get rid of it by passing it off to a coworker or supervisor.

17. Show some empathy or sympathy when a customer complains. Your doing or saying nothing when they feel they have a problem will put you in the doghouse fast.

18. Learn to say, "I apologize for what happened." Do something that will allow the customer to feel that you are apologizing. That quick, "Sorry 'bout that" statement sounds as though you're throwing the statement away.

19. Be prepared. If you're in customer service, or any front line position, expect things to happen. Being prepared is not just for the Boy Scouts. It's for anyone who works with customers. Prepare for the unexpected.

20. When in doubt, leave it out. Writing a letter to a client or calling them? If you're in doubt of using a certain word, leave it out or use something else.

21. This is reserved for you to put in your own customer service tip.

_____

_____

_____

_____

_____

_____

Do something "unexpected" for your customers.

Warning—Contagious Condition: Smilyosis

— Anonymous

There is an infectious condition that may run rampant through your office. It has been brought to our attention that many of you already have this condition, and that everyone is, at least, a carrier. Little is known about the history of the condition, but there is some evidence that it has persisted in humans for thousands of years. The condition is occasionally dormant in some persons and in apparent remission. A few people never show symptoms.

Experts indicate that the condition is highly contagious, but not always serious. In fact, for some people it may be beneficial. Statistics regarding the condition are difficult to develop as most cases go unreported.

The condition is most commonly passed by personal contact. You may catch it just by speaking with an infected person. Initial symptoms are so mild that you may not even realize you have been infected. Later, the condition may have more marked effects on you. Scientists also believe that the condition compounds itself, that is, the severity increases with increased exposure.

Experts also report that the condition can be transmitted in other ways. Reading a letter written by an infected person may create symptoms. Several cases have indicated instances where a single individual has infected large numbers of people through written material.

The condition is also commonly passed on by talking on the telephone with an infected person. Experts are not exactly sure how this happens, but symptoms have been observed in persons on the phone when no one else is near.

There is no known medical cure. The symptoms can be controlled to some extent, but most people refuse treatment. Interestingly, however, experts have observed numerous cases where a noninfected person has been able to temporarily alleviate all symptoms from an infected person with only minimal contact.

The initial symptoms are evidenced by an upturning of the ends of the mouth, often to the extent of showing one's teeth. The psychological effects can be very pronounced. The condition is often accompanied by a feeling of warmth (but not a fever) and happiness. Persons have been known to become almost euphoric during acute episodes. Many infected persons can be convinced to do almost anything and most find it difficult to be unkind or rude. The condition is called chronic infectious *smilyosis,* or more commonly, smiling.

If you encounter someone with this condition, there is little you can do—just smile!

> ## Smilyosis—catch it!

Telephone Service Tips

12 Timely Tips for Making an Effective Outbound Call

We all make outbound calls every day. Well, most of us do anyway. It's a process we take for granted, and because of that, some of us are far better at making outbound calls than others.

It's an *art,* not a science. But making a call to someone you don't know and having a conversation with that person is a skill. And we all know a skill is something that we can learn.

Here are 12 tips on making a more effective outbound call. Some are simple, and others are tricky. But then, all skills come with that caveat. Good luck!

1 Smile *before* you dial.

OK, you knew that was coming, didn't you? I can't say it any stronger than your mother did. Yes, a smile *can* be heard. And if it's not, it's one of the biggest turn-offs for you. That big grin (phony that it may be) needs to be in your voice before you even dial the number to reach the person. So what we're talking about here, in effect, is a good mental attitude. At the Telephone Doctor, we don't even want an employee coming into work if they're not in a good mood. Bottom line, your voice reflects how you feel. And if it's not feeling happy, enthusiastic, energetic, and motivational, the first few seconds of your opening will fall flat on its face. And believe me, you only get a few seconds to make that great impression on the phone—that's all. About 4 to 6 seconds for the introduction. If the intro isn't smiling (unless you're reporting the death of someone), you're starting off, as they say, on your left foot. ***Remember to smile before you dial!***

2 **End the day ready to begin.**

That always reminds me of my grandmother's saying, "Up the street, the soldiers are marching down." It's a little convoluted. But you know what it means. At the end of the day, you should have your "tomorrow calls" already set up on your desk and ready to call. It's a time waster to come in and then start looking for whom you should be calling. Take 10 or 15 minutes at the end of your day and stack a pile of calls or "To Do's" for yourself in the morning.

3 **Avoid being screened.**

I don't know about you, but I *hate* being screened. So I started to implement my own technique to avoid this, and now I *never* get screened. That's right: *never*. How would you like to never be screened? OK, listen up. It's important for you, as you read this, to know a little bit of my background. You see, I used to be a secretary and I know from experience, secretaries don't get up in the morning and think to themselves, "Oh goody, I get to screen people today." It's not like that. It's more like "Nancy, I want you to screen all my calls."

You see, secretaries are told to screen, and the truth is, most of them don't know how to effectively screen callers. So they end up with the old, "Who's calling?" "Who is this?" or even worse, "Will he know what this is about?"

Since (let's call her "Suzy") Suzy has been told to screen calls, and you know she's been told to screen, doesn't it make sense to "handle the objection" before it comes up? In other words, start the conversation like this: "Hi, my name is Nancy Friedman. I'm calling long distance from St. Louis with the Telephone Doctor. I need to speak with Brad." Give *full disclosure* at the top of the call.

So guess what? I never get screened! The good news is you can do it too. If the person you're trying to reach has told "Suzy" to find out who it is or who they're with and even why they're calling, you will be giving the "Suzys" of the world two of the three things they need. The chances are pretty good that they won't even go for the third part, that being "what is this in reference to?"

Giving *full disclosure* at the *top* of the conversation is the key to not being screened. It also puts you apart from the dozens of calls the person gets. It befriends the "Suzys" of the world and it creates credibility.

4 **Drop the four killer words.**

"Hi, how are ya?" Want to really bug someone you've never talked with before? Just use those four words. "Hi, how are ya?" It's social noise. Who really cares? And what would you do if someone replied, "Gee I'm so glad you asked. My migraines are getting worse, I've got a bad case of diarrhea, the pain in my knee is killing me, but the sores in my mouth are a lot better."

5 **Get a script and stick with it.**

Neil Simon, William Shakespeare, and a few other notable authors wrote plays. The actors stuck to the script. You should too. Don't go with Simon's or Shakespeare's of course. Bring your own. Put down on paper the thoughts or points you want to stress. That's a great way to keep your mind from going blank when you reach your contact.

There's a great secret to using your script, and that is to not sound like you're reading it. It needs to sound conversational. That takes practice, practice, and more practice. I suggest to the folks we train to practice into a tape recorder or even a video. Find out how you sound and look. Or practice phoning a friend or relative. Have them critique you. Tell them to "have no mercy." You need honest comments on how you sound. Having a script will keep the conversation within the boundaries it needs to be.

6 **Ask for time to talk.**

I'll keep this short, sweet, and to the point. Without asking if the party you called has a moment to talk, you are an interruption! We simply should never make a phone call without asking for time to talk. End of subject.

If it's not a good time for the contact, simply ask if later that day or tomorrow would be better for him or her. Or you can ask when a more convenient time would be. Remember that most people are doing something else when we call them. And our call *is* an interruption. Few of them are sitting at their desk, hands folded, waiting for your call.

7 Keep your productivity button up.

Do you know where your productivity button is? It's the receiver hook on the phone. If the receiver hook is down, you're not on the phone making calls and your productivity will go down as well. Batch your calls by time zones or however makes sense. If you've got a project that entails reaching 10 or 15 contacts, make one call after the other. Don't stop. Keeping your productivity button up keeps the momentum going.

8 Keep excellent notes on every call.

Keeping these notes short, sweet and to the point, will be a big help when you reach someone. If you've spoken to a helpful assistant, make a note to let the person know that. Be sure you also jot notes as the contact talks. This will allow you to go back and refresh your mind as well as the contacts. People think I have a great memory, all because I keep good notes and refer to them when needed. It's a nice touch.

9 Follow up when you say you will.

Man, is this important. If someone has told you when to call them back, be there or be square. That's an appointment and if it is missed, you lose lots of points. Even if you call them back when they have told you to and they're not there. At least you have kept your word and can leave a voicemail message that you did call. It's not nice to say you'll call someone on a certain day or time and then not do it. How can they trust you with the information if you're not even going to do what you said you would?

10 Use some sort of timer for reminders.

This tip connects to #9. A contact has asked you to call back in a few hours. I don't know about you, but my day gets pretty busy, and it's possible I could forget to call the contact back. But I don't forget. I use the small digital timer that's on my desk. I set it and forget it. When it buzzes I know I have a call to make. Even if I'm somewhere else in the office, my assistant calls me to say the alarm is going off. Today, with the computer reminders or cell phone alarms, it's much easier. One more thing, set the alarm for 5 or 10 minutes ahead of time to allow you to get your notes or refresh your memory before you dial.

11 Call a satisfied contact.

OK, you've hit 23 voicemails, three people didn't have time to talk with you, and two darn near hung up on you. Time to call someone you know and love, and more importantly, who knows and loves you. That's right. When you're down and out and you feel every call is going to be a bust, call a person who really has been a friend and likes you. Even if it's to leave a simple "Hi, I was thinking about you" voicemail message. It'll really lift your spirits (and his/hers).

12 Expect the called party not to be in.

Planning ahead is not just for the Boy Scouts. Anyone making phone calls needs to do the same thing. Plan ahead. Plan and expect the person you're trying to reach *not* to be there.

The Telephone Doctor surveys show that only 30 percent of all calls reach the intended party on the first try. Wow! That's not a great average. Voicemail has taken over, hasn't it? Be prepared to leave a *great* voicemail message. (The subject of voicemail messages is covered in other articles.) If you're leaving a message with a human being (and they're hard to find nowadays aren't they?), try to have the message *read back to you.* It's amazing how many messages read back to me are wrong. So if possible, ask the person if he/she can connect you to your contact's voicemail instead. At least that way you know that your message will be delivered verbatim.

Re-read number 6. It's *key.*

Controlling Personal Calls at the Office

Do you allow personal calls at the office? Let employees know your policy on personal phone calls. Develop a policy if you don't have one. Help your staff follow your rules by giving them specific guidelines. Here are a few suggestions:

- *Never* let an in-person customer wait while an employee is on a personal call. (Even if it's a business call, the customer should be acknowledged—even if it's only with a smile and a nod.)

- Sometimes employees just don't know how to tactfully tell a friend or relative they are at work and unable to talk. They may be embarrassed to tell them. Here's a Telephone Doctor tip on how to handle that graciously:

  > "Aunt Mary, I'd like to hear more about your trip, but I'm at work and need to get some things done for the boss. Let me call you later tonight when we can talk more in depth. Thanks for calling. Talk with you later."

- Let employees know that if they are approached by the boss (or other coworker), they are expected to put their personal call on hold. Personal calls can wait...office personnel shouldn't.

Encourage employees while on the phone with a customer to use the client's name during the call. It makes it easier for you and coworkers to realize it's a business call. (Using names also helps build rapport with a client.) There's not an intelligent manager around who would interrupt a business call.

**Don't take advantage of
your boss or your company.**

Do's and Don'ts of Executive Phone Skills

Why is it when the subject of telephone skills comes up most executives tune out? "Send the staff," they say. For whatever reason, there's a group of these folks who feel they're in that old ivory tower and exempt themselves from any type of telephone skills training.

There are definitely some fire breathing executives who need a class on phone skills—both inbound and outbound. There are no job title restrictions on this topic. Everyone within an organization should go through some sort of phone skills training.

Remember, it all starts at the top. It dribbles down; it cannot dribble up. So many management and top-level executives are guilty of exhibiting poor phone skills and probably only because the topic of phone skills is thought of as something reserved for frontline employees, when in fact, phone skills should start at the top!

Here, in no particular order, are some very valuable phone skills for everyone—especially executives and top level management.

- **DO** acknowledge all your phone calls. If you're unable to return a phone call yourself, at least have it returned on your behalf. Not returning a phone call is like not using your turn signal on the highway. Rude and sometimes dangerous.

- **DO** place your own phone calls. Or if you absolutely need to have someone else place a call for you, at least be ready when the person you called is on the line. It's legendary bad taste to have your assistant call someone and then put them on hold to wait for "Mr./Ms. Self-Important." Today, with speed dialing and auto dial, I see no valid reason to have an assistant dial a call for you and then turn the call over. Letting the assistant make the call and follow-through is fine. But do you have someone dial for you? That's a real *fagetaboutit.* (This goes for doing your own voicemail message too!)

- **DO** give bad news yourself. Not being able to deliver on time or canceling a contract is best given by you when at all possible. Having someone else deliver your bad news is what Telephone Doctor calls "distance induced bravery." And be careful about giving bad news on e-mail, as well. Bad news is best delivered face-to-face and/or on the phone directly with the person.

- **DO** identify yourself on accepting all incoming calls (even when you're using caller ID). Sometimes it's not who you "think" it is. There are horror stories about caller ID and it not being who you "think" it is. "Hello" isn't exactly a business greeting on the phone. Everyone likes to know who they're talking with...don't you? "Hi, this is Bob," will work fine. Please use your own name!

- **DO** expect your called party *not to be available.* Expect voicemail. Be prepared is not only for the Boy Scouts. Be prepared to leave a detailed message with full disclosure of who you are and how to reach you. **Bonus:** Leave your phone number twice...and slowly.

- **DON'T** make employees lie to your callers by having them say you're not there when you are or in a meeting when you're not. Face the music, or better yet, train your staff to handle the call. "Bob is in the office; however, unavailable. My name is Nancy. I work with him. How can I help you? What can I do for you?" It's much healthier than an out-and-out lie.

- **DON'T** be too busy to be nice. We're all busy. Being busy does not give you carte blanche to be rude.

- **DON'T** hide behind voicemail. It was not intended as a screening device or to warehouse calls.

- **DON'T** use a speakerphone on initial greetings. Echoy voices should not be the first thing a caller hears. Picking up on initial greeting on a speaker-phone says to the caller "I am too important to pick up the phone." And when you do need to use a speakerphone, it's a very nice thing to always ask the person on the other end of the line if he/she minds being on the speakerphone.

- **DON'T** use a cell phone for full-blown sales calls or presentations. There's too much chance for distrac-tion and, of course, an accident. And while we're on the subject of cell phones, I'm not sure why, but most folks seem to have a need to shout—and usu-ally at airports, restaurants, and social functions. Take your phone to a place where you're not dis-turbing everyone.

- **Bonus**: **DON'T** leave bad news on voicemail. You can leave a message saying you need to discuss a situation, but leaving bad news on voicemail is again, distance induced bravery.

**Re-read these tips.
They're valuable.**

Handling the Irate Customer

If your job entails taking calls from unhappy, irate customers, you've got your work cut out for you. Employees who deal with customers are especially vulnerable to outbursts from customers who are already going through an emotional, stressful time.

Handling these types of customers takes time and training, but it can be accomplished effectively. Here are some of the Telephone Doctor's best techniques for turning unhappy customers into satisfied customers.

Getting Off on the Right Foot

Realize that upset, angry customers are not unhappy with you, it's the situation. Don't take a customer's hostility personally. You are merely the lightening rod that redirects the violent lightening. You can do a great deal to diffuse a customer's anger before you ever pick up the phone. How? By smiling *before* you answer that call. You can really "hear" a smile over the phone. It's very difficult to be rude to someone who is warm and friendly.

Handling a Hostile Call

There are four basic steps to handling an irate customer. The Telephone Doctor calls them our ASAP technique:

A **Acknowledge** the person's feelings and apologize for the inconvenience the customer has encountered. Make an effort to be sincere. In today's impersonal society, it's incredibly rare to hear the words, *"I'm sorry that happened. Let me get the ball rolling to fix it."* You'll probably spend about 80 percent of your time massaging the customer's feelings and 20 percent actually solving the problem.

S **Sympathize** and empathize with the customer. Phrases like *"I can understand why you're upset"* can help soothe ruffled feathers. Pretend it's you calling. Then get busy solving the problem.

A **Accept** 100 percent responsibility for the call. This is probably the toughest part. Chances are excellent that you had nothing to do with the problem; however, it's your job to take the responsibility and help initiate a solution.

P **Prepare** to help. Begin by re-introducing yourself. Customers don't usually remember your name. State that you will be able to help. Use the customer's name, if possible. This helps to diffuse anger. A willing attitude is essential, because if the customer senses insincerity or indifference, it will cause them to stay angry. It's exasperating to file a complaint with someone who obviously doesn't care.

The ASAP technique works! Try it and see!

Not Making Excuses

Never make an excuse to a complaining customer. No one wants to hear *"The computer is down"* or *"I'm the only one here."* That is your problem, not the customer's. When you give an excuse, the customer automatically hears *"I'm not going to help you."*

Transferring Calls

Sometimes you're not able to solve the problem on the spot. Many times you need more information from another department. Perhaps the call needs to be handled by another person. Although these are legitimate courses of action, they usually upset your customer all over again.

If you need more information, *tell* the customer. Ask the customer if he/she is able to hold while you obtain the information or if he/she would prefer a call back. *"Joe, I need to check with our claims department in order to answer your question. It will take two or three minutes. Are you able to hold/wait while I check?"* Avoid untrue phrases like *"Hold on a second."* Nothing takes a second.

If you need to transfer a caller, let the caller know the name of the person with whom he/she will be speaking. Give a reason why you're bringing in a third party. *"Joe, Mrs. Smith in our claims department is the real expert in resolving your type of situation. Let me transfer you directly to her."*

**Irate customers are no fun;
but turning them into fans of
your business sure is!**

Have You Called You Yet?

If you're in business—and haven't taken the time to call up and ask for yourself, a service, or your product—that's your first assignment from the Telephone Doctor. You need to do just that. We cannot fix what we do not know.

Not to know how your customers are being handled is a cardinal sin. Call your business and see how your customers are treated. If you're satisfied fine, but I can tell you after years of interviewing and working with thousands of large and small business owners, very few are satisfied with how their phones are answered.

Do we take phone answering for granted? Sure we do. Hey, Helen's not here today, get someone in here to grab the phones. Get someone in here? To grab the phones? There's not a business person alive that will disagree with the fact that: *The first person who answers the phone is the voice of the company. The company representative. The voice of management...* blah blah blah. Then why on earth would you let just "anyone come in and grab the phones"?

So now that we're all in agreement that the phones at your business are critical to the success of your business, what are we going to do? Here's what the Telephone Doctor will tell you to do. Whoever answers your phone *is the company.* The owner, the boss, the wife of the boss, the daughter, or whoever can be that first person. So what we are trying to tell you is: *Whoever answers the phone is responsible for the business.*

Fact: *Answering phones isn't just for women anymore.* Nah, you guys need to take the brunt too. I can tell you that I've heard about some fire-breathing executives, both male and female, who misuse the telephone.

143

If you have answered the phone on behalf of your company, you have indeed accepted 100 percent responsibility for that phone call.

Probably the most often asked question I get when speaking at a conference is, "Hey, Nancy, what's the best way to answer the phone?" Well, I'm not sure I know the only way, but I sure do know the **most effective way.** Here's our Telephone Doctor three-part greeting.

When answering a business phone, you only need three things:

1. **A Buffer:** This can be Good Morning, Good Afternoon, Thanks for Calling, Merry Christmas, Happy Tuesday, etc. I don't care what the buffer is, it just needs to be there. Buffer words are the welcoming words that say to your caller, "I'm so glad you called!" Without buffer words, the name of the company is cold and uncaring. So use buffers to warm the call. Also, buffer words set up the most important part of any conversation, which in this case is going to be your company name. So again, use buffers.

2. **Your Company Name (or Department Name):** When you use buffers, it slows you down a tad and allows the company name, the most important part of the greeting, to be heard.

3. **Your Name:** Use it with "This is": "This is Nancy." "This is Jan." "This is Bob." Do not use "Betty speaking." Betty Speaking is married to Tom Speaking. They have three kids—Billy Speaking, Andy Speaking, and Tommy Speaking. People will remember the last thing you say on the greeting; we'd like it to be your name!

Personal Note: "How can I help you?" is *not necessary* on initial greetings. You are there to help! Why else would you answer the phone? These words are useless in an initial greeting. "How can I help you" should be used within message taking scenarios.

So it's like this: "Hi! Thanks for calling Telephone Doctor, This is Nancy." Stop! Anything after your name erases your name. And your name at the end speeds the rapport-building process.

OK, there you have it. And it's so simple. We haven't even gone into the *tone* of the voice, the smile, and a few other things that go into the initial greeting. But if you're looking to have your customers say, "Hey, that sounds super," use the Telephone Doctor's three-part greeting!

Call your own office and ask for yourself, a service, or a product. How'd they handle it?

How to Deal with the Foreign Accent

Call it simple kindness or call it common sense, but learning to deal with foreign accents can definitely be good for business.

More than one million immigrants enter the United States each year, most with one thing in common, difficulty expressing themselves clearly in English. Foreigners, however, represent a sizable market for any corporation marketing products or services in the United States.

To help serve this growing group of customers effectively, following is the Telephone Doctor's five-point program on dealing with the foreign accent over the telephone.

1 **Don't pretend to understand.**

If you don't understand the person you're speaking with, it's perfectly OK to gently tell them you're having a little bit of difficulty understanding them. If they could slow down just a little bit, you'd be able to get all the information correct. That's what they want to hear. Hanging up without knowing what the caller wanted is not good customer service.

2 **Don't rush.**

Rushing threatens callers. Take the time to do it right. It usually takes only a few extra seconds. Listen to the caller's pattern of speech. You'll be able to pick up key words. Repeat the key words back to them. They'll appreciate the fact that you're really listening.

147

3 Don't shout.

Like the old joke goes, people with foreign accents aren't hard of hearing. Nor do you need to repeat one word over and over and over to be sure they understand.

4 Don't be rude.

We usually don't mean to be rude when talking with someone with a foreign accent. However, if you've ever told someone "I can't understand you," or even "What did you say?" you've been a little bit rude. It's much better to stop, take full responsibility and explain you're having a little difficulty understanding them and if they could repeat themselves again, you'll be able to assist. Subtle little differences, but key ones.

5 Do keep a job aid available.

If you're receiving calls from one ethnic group more than another, keep a handy job aid near your phone. All you need are a few common phrases to get you off the hook. For example, in Spanish even, "un momento por favor" poorly pronounced by you would be appreciated by someone who's having difficulty trying to get something over the phone. You can then bring someone to the phone who will be able to assist.

These techniques can be equally beneficial when communicating with people who have regional accents and even senior citizens.

**Remember: Those with an
accent are not hard of hearing.**

How to Handle Call *Reluctance* and Call *Rejection*

A while back at a sales training program I delivered, an insurance salesman told me he had "call reluctance" and asked how to handle it.

I was slightly taken aback. I really couldn't imagine a salesperson having call reluctance and being successful. That's what I call an oxymoron. The two just don't go together.

Call reluctance, the fear of picking up the phone, is obviously not a great characteristic of a successful salesperson. On the other hand, I can fully understand and can successfully treat "call rejection."

Well, you're asking, what's the difference between the two? Big time difference, my friend, big time.

If you feel you happen to have call reluctance, meaning you're obviously reluctant to pick up the phone and make a call, why not start with little steps. Call for information at a local store. Call friends and talk with them. Try calling folks you haven't heard from in a while. Hopefully, the fear of picking up the phone will be erased, and you'll be able to move forward.

I'm not sure how to fix call reluctance, or even if it can be. However, I am very sure how to fix call rejection. So as Telephone Doctor always likes to do, let's focus on the positive and help you handle call rejection—the fear of being rejected by your customers.

The number one reason a salesperson has call rejection is because he's unsure about his product. He may not have all the answers to the objections he knows he'll get.

Call rejection is a form of FUD. That's right, F-U-D. Don't bother looking it up in the dictionary. It's not there. We made it up, but it's something every professional salesperson has dealt with at one time or another: FUD—fear, uncertainty, and doubt.

Fear. Since we know fear is often from lack of product knowledge, we also know it can be fixed. Study up on your company, your industry, your product, your competitors; anything you can do to be sure you understand exactly what it is you're doing, selling, and talking about.

Once you're secure in that area, some, if not all, of the fear will disappear. Think of a 2- or 3-year-old child taking his first swimming lesson. Most kids (OK, OK not yours!) are very fearful of putting their head and face into the water. Why? Because they don't know how; they don't know anything about it. But then they learn how to do it safely. And guess what? They swim. They had a form of call rejection. They had "swim rejection." Same principle.

So learn all you can about your industry, your company, and your competitors. It will help reduce, if not cure, your fear of being rejected and your customer's fear about choosing the right product/vendor.

Uncertainty. Right. What's going to happen? If you're in sales, you may have heard the old saying, "Nothing happens till someone sells something." Or perhaps the other old saying, "Every *no* is one step closer to a *yes.*"

There are probably a lot more of those sayings, but bottom line, if you've learned about your company, industry, and competitors, then we're just uncertain about the outcome, right? Uncertain of what someone will say.

To help handle the uncertainty, make a list of all the possible objections you might hear—whatever they are. Write them down. Then jot down the answers to those objections. Keep the list in front of you while you're on the phone so that you're prepared. When the customer says:

- "I'm not ready" or
- "I can't afford it" or
- "It's too expensive" or
- "That's 2 percent more than the other guy."

Whatever the objection might be, you'll have an answer ready. Example:

- **I'm not ready.** *Possible answer:* "Well, let me ask you this Mr. Prospect, when do you feel you will be ready?"

- **I can't afford it.** *Possible answer:* "If I can show you a way that you can afford it, will you be open to listening?"

- **It's too expensive.** *Possible answer:* "Tell me how expensive you feel it is."

- **That's 2 percent more than the other guy.** *Possible answer:* "Right, we are. And do you happen to know why that is?" (Then be prepared to show them.)

It's a rare salesperson who can bring up the immediate answer to every objection on the spot. Oh yes, there are some, but most of us are limited to what we can remember. By writing down all the possible objections and all the answers to them, you immediately remove the "uncertainty" in FUD. You have the information right in front of you!

Doubt. Now comes the "D" in FUD: doubt. Doubt is usually what the buyer has. Are you the right broker? Is your company the best? The most well known? The most respected? Is my money secure?

Once you have mastered fear and uncertainty, you'll eliminate the doubt in your customer's mind by your confidence and knowledge of your product. It's the non-confident salesperson who brings doubt to a customer.

So bottom line: Overcoming call rejection can be fixed. Make up *your* mind to fix what's wrong.

You can do it. There's no FUD about that!

You can make a great living making cold calls.

How *Not* to Answer a Telephone Call

Throughout the years, our Telephone Doctor clients have taken the time to jot us a note to let us know about their good experiences and their not-so-good experiences of how they've been treated on the telephone. I expect, judging from the amazing number of entries we received for our book *Customer Service Nightmares*, it's a way of venting and releasing their frustration. We're always happy to receive your notes and e-mails. Keep them coming, please.

The recent e-mail below gave us some good ammunition for an article. While the industry, as you can see, is in the legal profession, believe me, it happens all the time in every industry. Read on:

Around 1:00 p.m. today I returned opposing counsel's telephone call from this morning. The first person who answered the phone took my name and asked me to hold while he checked to see if she was back from lunch. After a short hold he came back on the line and transferred my call. At that point opposing counsel's assistant answered the phone. She took my name for the second time and put me back on hold. After holding a couple of minutes, opposing counsel's assistant came back on the line and asked if I could call back in 20 minutes! I am sure that her assistant is telling opposing counsel that I am a jerk because I answered, "No, I am calling her back now."

Unbelievable. Makes me wonder how they handle calls from their clients.

It's not important to know the "who" in this story. It's more important to learn the "why" it happened. And more importantly, how to fix it! That's what this article is about.

It's a well-known fact that the first voice you hear when you call a company sets the tone, makes the first impression, and welcomes the caller. It starts the rapport-building factor. Few will argue that point.

While there are several faux pas in the e-mail above, which is the *major* one? Reread it and see if you don't agree with Telephone Doctor mentality, culture, and philosophy. Our answer is at the end of this article.

In the meantime, it sounds as though the opposing counsel's office can use a dose of our *Basic Basic Telephone Skills* program. Listed below are a few key points from our popular DVD program *Basic Basic Telephone Skills*. Know anyone else who might benefit from this list?

1. While we didn't get to find out *how* they answer the phone with their initial greeting, we hope they used the Telephone Doctor three-part greeting. A buffer, the company name, and then their name. Remember, "How can I help you" is *not* necessary in initial greetings. You are there to help. That is why you answered the phone.

2. Learn how to put a caller on hold. "Hold on," CLICK is not effective. Neither is "Hang on a second." Several years ago, we ran a survey with *USA Today* to find out what frustrates the caller the most. *Yes, being put on hold was the number one frustration of the American public.* That was 12 years ago. Today, it's number three with, yes—you guessed it—the automated attendant being number one!

3. Monogram the call. If the caller lets you know his/her name, *use it.* Immediately.

4. Leave a good lasting impression. Seems as though the opposing counsel's office didn't do that. Remember we'll tell more people about a bad experience than we will a good one. We're not sure why, but it is true.

What was the worst faux pas? Asking a caller to call back! We never ask anyone to call back. That's like kicking a customer out of the door at the store. When someone calls us, it's our job to return the call, or have it returned on our behalf. Asking someone to call back is just rude. (Exception: there are times when the caller will say, "Let her know I called and I'll call back." That's fine if it's the caller's choice. But to ask a caller to please call back... Wow! *Big mistake.* That's a real no no!

You can ruin the entire phone event with poor answering.

Monogram the Call

Think of all the items you use that have your initials or even your name on them. And have you ever given a gift and had a name or initials put on it? Most likely you have. Certainly, you've seen monograms on a variety of items. And we know that many catalog companies encourage us to have a monogram embroidered on an item.

So what does that have to do with customer service in your organization? Glad you asked. Has this ever happened to you? You're in the grocery store pushing that cart to the checkout. The cashier appears to do a good job scanning your things. She (or he) tells you the total—$115. (I just went in for butter, milk, and eggs.) You pull out the checkbook, make the check out for $115 exactly, hand over the check, and...*nothing*. Oh, wait. Something did happen. The bagger asked you if you would like paper or plastic.

What didn't happen here was no one *monogrammed* or used your name during the event. You gave the cashier your check—*with your name on it* (address and phone number too), and she still didn't monogram the event. She didn't use your name. She had it, but didn't use it. Had you given her cash, you might have been more understanding. (We seldom, if ever, put our name on cash.) Yes, you gave her your name, and she didn't use it!

Know the name? Use the name! It's that simple. When you're lucky enough to be given the customer's name, please use it. It makes the entire transaction a little friendlier and a little easier to handle, and it shows you care.

The difference is very apparent. I was in line to board a plane the other day, and the person taking the tickets used the name of every single passenger. And yes, with a big smile. Because it's done so rarely, it made a big impression on me. Hey, I gave her my name, and by golly, she used it.

On the telephone, you won't get handed anything with a name on it, but chances are you'll have every opportunity to get a name and then use the name. You'll be able to "monogram" the call.

Listening skills come into play here as evidenced by something that happened to me recently. I made a phone call, introduced myself and the reason for the call, and the next thing out of the person's mouth was: "Name?" I told him it was still "Nancy." I hadn't changed it from seven seconds before.

So the question becomes, "What do we do when someone gives us a name and we miss it?" Good question! The Telephone Doctor has a great technique for getting that name you missed.

It's easy. Someone gives you his or her name and then continues on with the conversation. Unless you've written it down, you've probably forgotten it. So we take control of the call and say, "I know you said your name, and I apologize, I missed it. My name is Nancy. And you are?"

What we've done here is take responsibility of the situation. And we covered the objection ahead of time: admitting the caller said their name and yet we missed it. It's a real crowd pleaser.

So, remember—**know** the name? **Use** the name.

> ### Know the name?
> ### Use the name!

Returning Phone Calls

I'm often asked: "Nancy, what do you think of people who don't return phone calls?"

My answer is a quick and simple, "Not very much."

Not returning a phone call or have it returned in your behalf? Few things can be labeled as "ruder." (Worse?) Then I hear, "Yes, but Nancy, you just don't know how many calls I get during the day. I just can't return them all."

We all get a lot of phone calls, myself included. And I may not be able to return each and every call myself; however, I do make sure they get returned on my behalf by someone in the office.

True story: A while back, I was cleaning up my office (no comments, please) and moved a file cabinet. Lo and behold I found a phone message from about eight months prior. The message had slipped behind the cabinet and obviously I had not returned the call. I immediately stopped what I was doing and called the person. When he answered, I told him, "You know I always return my calls. I just never say when." Fortunately, because he was a good friend, he totally understood when I explained the situation to him. And fortunately, too, it hadn't been a high-priority call.

Not returning a phone call is like not using your turn signal: just plain rude. The other day, my husband and I were driving down the highway and one of the cars went from lane to lane to lane without using the turn signal. Dick looked at me and said, "Well, he probably doesn't return his phone calls, either."

"Ah....Nancy, but what if it's an unhappy customer? I don't like to return those calls." My answer: "You're getting the proverbial second chance. The customer is letting you know something is wrong and would like you to fix it." It's when the customer *never* calls back that you need to be concerned about. That's when they're taking their business somewhere else.

Voicemail tip: Be careful when you put "I'll call you back by 5:00" (or whenever) on your voicemail. There may be things that prevent you from calling back when you say you will, and then you've not lived up to your promise. Give yourself some breathing time when you make a promise to return a call.

Telephone Doctor Tip: Return all phone calls or have them returned on your behalf.

Reminder: Someone called you. It's nice to call them back or have the call returned on your behalf.

Service after the Sale

This is a true story: Early in the year, we put out a bid for a printing job, and several firms came forth to give us a quote. One even came out to the office with a personal quote. He seemed so interested and appreciative of the opportunity to work with us.

While his firm wasn't the lowest bid, it wasn't the highest. Because he was right there in the middle and because he just didn't fax us a quote, we decided to give him the business. After all, there was more to gain here for him because we do a lot of printing.

The job was done quickly and done right. He even called to be sure we were happy. "Yes," we told him, "it looked great. Thanks for the good job."

Six months later, I received a call from the same salesperson asking why he hadn't heard from us with other bids. "Excuse me?" I asked, "Is it my responsibility to check up on you? Where have you been for the past six months? Why would I call you when I hadn't heard from you again?" "Point well taken," he said.

I then related a story I had from one of my recent speaking engagements at a printing association. At the end of my programs, time permitting, I like to add a Q & A session. One man raised his hand and asked me, "How can I get my clients to call me before they run out?" I honestly couldn't believe he asked that. Without missing a beat, I told him it was his responsibility to call the customer and be sure everything was alright. Catch them *before* they run out, so they don't have an opportunity to call another printer. "Yeah, I guess you're right," he said.

Of course I'm right, but that's not the point. How in the world can you sell someone something, let six months go by without contacting them, and then call them to find out why they haven't called you? What's wrong with that picture?

Here's another true story from one of our Telephone Doctor account executives. Naturally we're a bit more customer service oriented than most, so certain things stand out. Danny called a cleaning company to have his carpets cleaned, and an appointment was made for the company to be there on Friday. To make a long story short, no one ever showed.

On Saturday, the cleaning company called and left a voicemail message on his machine, requesting that *he* call them Monday and allow them to apologize and reschedule. "Right," thought Danny, "don't hold your breath for that call."

The cleaning company had Danny's cell phone number. They should have tracked him down or told him on his machine that they will continue to try to reach him.

What's wrong with these companies? Don't they understand the process? If you are selling something, it is your responsibility to call the customer. You are lucky when the customer calls you back.

In this day and age, with companies struggling for customer loyalty, here is a spot where you can rise above the average. Be proactive. Make a reminder or tickler file to make contact with your customers. Certainly I'm a proponent of a phone call. However, I would have been happy with an "anytime" card—a card or note we send for no special reason, just to say hello, any time of the year—from that printer. The printer we use now stops in to visit with us once or twice a quarter. He also sends a plate of sandwiches for the entire office once a year. He does these things because he wants his name in our memory bank when it's time to reorder.

Why would we call someone who hasn't contacted us? Why wouldn't we call someone who has kept their name in front of us so that when it's time to reorder, we naturally think of them?

Learn to make what the Telephone Doctor calls a "no ulterior motive" call. They're wonderful. You simply call the client and tell them, "This is a no ulterior motive call, just a genuine hello and thanks for being a great customer." Eight out of 10 times, the client will say, "I'm glad you called...we need such and such." Even if they don't order anything, guess who they'll think of when they need something in your industry?

Customer service isn't just being nice when you sell something, it's a process. It's a lifetime of wanting to have the customer only think of you. It's a phone call, a card, or a note. It is *not* calling a client up and wondering why they haven't called *you.*

Service after the sale...a forgotten skill. Call or write your customer after you've taken the money.

Telephone Inquiries are *Not* Always About Price
(How to Capture the Call)

P   PREPARE to be PROACTIVE. Remember: To gain information on the phone, you need to give information. Reintroduce yourself again to the caller.

R   REASSURE your callers that they have come to the right place. Thank them for the call. Explain you'll be of help and all you need to do is ask them a few necessary questions to be sure you're going to fill their needs. Remember to use the caller's name if you have it.

I   INTEGRITY. Stress quality, service, professionalism, and confidentiality. Full disclosure of price, product, and service to the caller promotes honesty. Be consistently sensitive to the caller's needs.

C   CALM, COOL, CONFIDENCE. This is the time to let the caller know you care.

E   EXCEED the caller expectations. Do something special. Offer more information than they request.

> **Price answers should come at the end of the conversation, not the beginning.**

165

The Three-Part Greeting

Hundreds of thousands of dollars are leaking through the phone lines at businesses in corporate America, both large and small, because of how people answer the telephone. Whether the initial call comes in through the switchboard or at the executive's desk, anyone who answers the phone is responsible for handling that call. Executives across the country as well as frontline support people all need some sort of training to greet the caller.

Simple and basic as it sounds, most businesses don't pay much attention to the initial greeting of a phone call. Your voice, your tone of voice, and the words you use are critical in the first four to six seconds—because that's all you get to make a good impression on the telephone.

How do you answer your telephone? Or better yet, how does your staff answer it? If you don't know, pick up the phone, call your office, and ask for yourself, a service, or a product. If you don't like what you hear, it's time to call the doctor, the Telephone Doctor that is. At home, "hello" may suffice, but in the business world, it doesn't cut the mustard. To create a good impression, use the Telephone Doctor's three-part greeting.

PART 1: The Buffer

That's the soft welcoming mat that welcomes the caller into your business. Some common buffers are, "Good Morning," "Thank you for calling," "We're glad you called," "Happy holidays," "Happy Tuesday"—anything that says "thanks for calling." Buffer words set up the most important part of the conversation, and that is your company name.

PART 2: Company or Department Name

Without the buffer, your company or department name becomes hard and cold. Buffer words can be cut off, your company or department name should not be. Have you ever called a company and heard, for example, "ank..." when the person on the other end of the line really said "First National Bank"? Because the mouthpiece wasn't up to the mouth, part of the company name got cut off. Company or department names should be said confidently and clearly, not rushed and mumbled.

PART 3: Your Name

Every phone has a name, and if you're answering it, it should be yours. Giving your name helps speed the rapport-building process. If anyone asks, "Who's this?" you've answered the phone ineffectively. You sign your letters, sign your phone calls.

Ineffective initial greetings can cost businesses many lost dollars. Effective initial greetings create good will and start the conversation off on the right foot. Mix together the three parts and serve with a big smile: "Good morning, XYZ Company, this is Nancy."

By the way, "How can I help you?" is not necessary on the initial greeting. You are there to help; that's why you've answered the phone.

Use the Telephone Doctor's three-part greeting to get your business going right!

Remember, "How can I help you" is **not** necessary in the initial greeting.

Human Resources Tips

Back to Basics: Hiring the Right Voice

It's a well-known fact: That first voice callers hear when they call a company sets the tone—makes the first impression—and welcomes callers. Few will argue that point.

Sadly, one of the most important and overlooked techniques for hiring people who are going to be answering the phones for your company is not done as often as it should be. And that is to interview them by phone first. That's right. If you're interviewing for someone to handle your calls, have them call you and talk with them *before* you bring them to the office to do the interview.

- A good way to start is simply: "Tell me about yourself." If the candidates have any difficulty talking about the one topic they should know the most about, how will they be able to talk about your company?

- Be on the look out for those candidates who only answer your questions with one-word answers like "Yes" or "No." One-word answers are considered cold and unfriendly. And listen to hear the tone of their voice. You, as owners and managers, know you can hear a smile. Is it there? If it's not there at this point, chances are, it never will be. The old adage about first impressions is so true, especially in the interview.

- You'd be much better off with an over-enthusiastic individual who needs to "tone down" than to have a mild, unenthusiastic person who needs to be "tuned up." Tell the candidate at the time of your phone

171

interview to be the best they can be, because this will determine if they get a second, personal interview. Since the job consists primarily of being on the phone, it's an excellent way to "test" a candidate.

- Don't be surprised or disappointed if you run through several candidates before one comes up that will have the credentials you need. Just keep at it. Don't lower your standards just because you're busy. Once you do, the competition has an edge over you.

- Once candidates have passed the initial screening, what the Telephone Doctor calls the "smile test," then you can ask them to come in for further interviewing. At that point, you can give them the other important skill testing you need to do. Remember, most of the calls they will be taking are from people who will never see them. However, they should still be clean and well-kept with a great smile and great attitude.

Below are some of the questions you might want to ask candidates in an interview for a customer service position:

- **How long can you stay in one area and still be comfortable?** Since this position usually requires staying in one area, answering phones, and not running all over the office, ask them to tell you about the times they needed to stay in one area and how it made them feel. If the applicant likes to be all over the office, it may not be a good match.

- **How do you handle conflicting priorities?** There might be times when the person answering the phones may be asked to do some 'nonessential' jobs (i.e., folding letters, stuffing envelopes). The candidates must understand "you cannot do two things well at once." Be sure they know the phone is a priority and the folding and stuffing can hold. The callers shouldn't!

- **How do you feel about the position?** How important is answering the phones to you? When we feel something is important, we will do much better at that job. Let the candidate tell, and sell, you on how key the customer service position is for your company. (In other words, don't tell them how important it is...let them tell you.)

- **How much telephone training have you had in the past?** Where and what? Get specific. Employees who value training will be good ones for you and they will want to continue being trained. They will expect to be trained. It's a known fact that employees feel more secure in their position when they have been trained. They realize and appreciate that your time and money is being spent on them. Training is good job insurance for both parties.

Unfortunately, not everyone is a good candidate for answering phones. Please don't just hire someone, sit them in an area with the phones, and tell them, "OK, now be nice." They will need to know how you want it done. Answering phones is an art, not a science.

Before offering phone training, carefully consider the following: How do you want your phones to be answered? Company name only? What about a "Good morning" or "Thanks for calling"? How about using the name of the person who answers the phone? Is there a company standard? How are calls transferred? Is voicemail an option? Are all employees well trained on the system? Answering these questions prior to training will help you teach new employees exactly how you would like the phones answered.

Telephone skills training should not be ignored. And yet, it oftentimes is. Unfortunately, customer service positions are usually lower paying positions. They shouldn't be. Employ people with good work ethics and a happy attitude and pay them well. It will be well worth it for you and your company.

Be sure your voice of choice represents you well.

"Carol Doesn't Work Here Anymore"

A few years ago, I interviewed and subsequently hired a woman for a position on the phones at our office. Needless to say, at the Telephone Doctor, our techniques are a condition of employment.

In this particular case, the young woman I interviewed was spectacular. She said the right thing. She looked right. She was the most positive, upbeat, happy individual I'd seen in a long time. We laughed and had a wonderful interview. Her laugh seemed contagious. Her beautiful smile was constant. Her positive mental attitude was perfect. She had faced much adversity in her life and she explained how she handled it with the same great mentality.

Her name was Carol. Needless to say, I was impressed. After she left, I thought about her: "Gee, what a special person this could be for us." Carol came back a day or so later for the second interview. Again, the same wonderful personality. Her friendliness was so natural, so outgoing that you wanted to bottle it. Bingo—I hired Carol on the spot. We were all very excited.

She went into our training program with gusto. She learned the product quickly, and after three or four weeks, we put Carol on the phones to call our clients.

One day shortly after she was put on the phones, I was walking past her office. I paused to listen to her. I was sure she'd be great. Well, I almost fell over. Here was the same woman, but her entire personality had changed. The voice I heard was downbeat, almost depressing. There sure was no smile in her voice. The conversation she had going with a client was stilted and cold. She gave only one-word answers. It was, to put it mildly, shocking and, frankly, embarrassing.

I quickly called Carol into my office. "Carol," I said, "what happened? When we interviewed you a few weeks ago, you were wonderful. You were so cheerful, so happy, and so full of life. Your voice had a personality I wanted to bottle. And now, while I was listening to you, it seemed as though you were an entirely different person. Your voice was down, there was no personality. You seemed cold and unfriendly. What happened?"

"Oh," she said without missing a beat and very firmly, "when we interviewed—that's different. We're like friends. That was fun. These are business calls. That's different."

"Wrong," I said, "these are our business friends and need to be treated as such." I told her if she was going to give me "half her personality," I'd give her half pay.

P.S.—Carol doesn't work here anymore.

Think about your interview. Did you tell the boss you loved people? That you loved to be busy? That you were a "people" person? Did you smile during the interview to impress him or her? Why be any different to your customers? Remember, they are your business friends and deserve the same treatment as you promised in that "great" interview you gave.

Be you. Be the person they interviewed: all the time. Don't be a "Carol."

Would you hire you?

I Think You Let the Wrong 400 Go!

Years ago, I was at a very well-known hotel in Atlantic City. From the moment I checked in, I knew something wasn't right. In fact, it was all wrong.

The check-in process was so very unpleasant—from no smiles, to not talking to me, to the bellman complaining how bad things were. This unpleasantness continued throughout my stay. It was one of those bad dream experiences.

Determined to find out what was wrong, since I couldn't believe a place so revered could be that bad, I searched up and down the hall looking for any employee I could talk to about the situation. None were to be found: not a housekeeper, not a security guard, no one.

I went to the business floor, where I felt surely someone in "authority" would be around, and still I found no one. Finally, I saw a gentleman coming my way. I walked faster to meet up with him to see if he was a hotel employee. Yes, he was! I could just make out the little gold bar with his name and department. Great!

"Pardon me," I said, "I'd like to ask a question. I know this is a well-known property and I need to tell you that the service here has been terrible. Check-in was very bad and it went downhill from there. You're with the hotel, can you tell me why the service is so bad here?"

"Well," he said, almost smiling, "we've downsized and 400 people were let go." Without missing a beat I told him, "I think you let the wrong 400 go."

In these challenging times, now is *not* the time to abandon your communication and people skills. Downsizing your staff should not result in downsizing the quality of service your customers receive. Your best weapon in today's competitive marketplace will be how you treat your customers.

Should you find your company in a downsizing situation, stress to your remaining staff how vitally important they are to the company's success. Obviously, they're important—they're the ones you kept! When your staff takes pride in their jobs and their company, that pride can translate into better performance and better service to your customers.

Of course, downsizing is difficult, but if you'll make sure you keep the "right 400" and keep them focused on good communication and people skills, you'll maintain your quality service standards as well as your business's reputation.

Train who you have.

Top 30 Reasons New Salespeople Don't Succeed

1. They don't know their skills.
2. They're not flexible.
3. They're not team players.
4. They don't use their sense of humor.
5. They don't use their imagination.
6. They don't listen to management.
7. They make no effort.
8. They get too comfortable, too fast.
9. They interrupt too often.
10. They don't ask enough open-ended questions.
11. They make too many assumptions.
12. They're not sales minded.
13. They're not able to handle corrective criticism.
14. They don't have enough enthusiasm.
15. They have poor time management skills.
16. They don't use their personality.
17. They don't have a "Whatever It Takes" mentality.
18. They lose their focus.
19. They're not able to deal with personality conflicts.
20. They don't truly believe in their product.
21. They don't understand rapport building.
22. They don't understand ongoing customer service.
23. They have too many unqualified leads.
24. They lack confidence.

25. They don't have long-term commitments.
26. They're short sighted.
27. Honesty is a problem for them.
28. They don't do any self-improvement.
29. They refuse to follow scripts.
30. They don't understand this list.

When you're through learning...you're through. There's always something to learn.

Voice Mail, E-Mail, and Cell Phone Tips

5 Most Frustrating Voicemail Phrases

Voicemail is always a source of frustration in the busy business world. And it's not just voicemail; the automated attendant is also on the frustration list. To help reduce voicemail frustration due to your office phone as well as your cell phone voicemail, here are the five most frustrating phrases and aspects of voicemail messages that your callers *don't* want to hear or experience.

1 "I'm not at my desk right now."

What a boring statement! Let your callers know where you *are*...not where you are not. Tell them, "I *am* in the office all this week" or "I'm in a sales meeting until 3 p.m." Let them know if you do or do not check messages.

2 "Your call is very important to me (us)."

This statement is a big time waster. The caller is thinking, "Well, if I'm so darned important, where the heck are you?" And then again, think about it. Maybe the call isn't so important to you. You just don't need this phrase.

3 "I'm sorry I missed your call."

How dull. Of course you're sorry (although, there are probably some calls that you're not sorry to have missed). Leave this phrase out. It's a given. Use the time and space for something more valuable, such as where you are and when you will return, or another contact they can call for information or assistance.

4 "I'll call you back as soon as possible."

This statement is not interesting and not fun, and based on Telephone Doctor surveys, it is probably not true. The truth is that most people aren't returning their phone calls in a timely fashion. If you're telling your callers you'll call them back, make sure you do. If you think you might not return the call, then try this: "Go ahead and leave your phone number and I'll *decide* if I'll call you back or not." (Just kidding!) Unreturned phone calls rank high on the frustration list. "As soon as possible" is not an effective phrase. All you need is to say, "I will call you back." (Then do it! Or have the call returned on your behalf.)

5 No escape.

Remember to offer your callers an escape from what we call "voicemail jail." Tell callers on your voicemail message to press zero for the operator if they need more information. Or better yet, give them the name and extension of someone else who can help them. However, many times their voicemail will come on also (then the caller will be in voicemail jail). The main point here is to offer an alternative if you're not at your desk. Plus, you've bought back some time to say something more interesting or helpful to the caller. (Escape might not apply to cell phones.)

Let's talk about voicemail in general. Voicemail, per se, has three parts: the automated attendant, the greeting your callers hear, and the message you leave for someone on their voicemail.

The Automated Attendant (or as many refer to it, "The Groaner")

The voice of the automated attendant is for many people the primary frustration with voicemail, especially when they are unable to get out of the system (i.e., no escape). The automated attendant was not installed to replace people. It was installed to (1) answer on the first ring, and (2) expedite a phone call. And it does do both. That being said, it's still a big frustration in the business world. Make it less frustrating for your callers!

Is there anyone reading this right now who would argue against the fact that the first voice you hear when you call a company sets the mood and tone for all future interactions? Then why on Earth would you leave a robotic, monotone, dull voice to greet your callers? Don't think you have to use the voice (or digital chip) that came with your system. There are options for you to record the message using your voice or the voice of one of your employees with a great, upbeat voice or that of a professional. You want a voice that says, "Hey, we're so glad you called." You want a greeting that is warm and friendly.

The Greeting on Your Voicemail

A reminder: People want to know where you are—not where you're not! It's pretty simple. Leave an escape for callers—some place they can get information if needed.

As for recording your greeting daily with the date, you might want to think twice about this. It's not wrong or bad to do this, but I think there are too many ways to slip up and not record each day, thereby making your greeting outdated. And an outdated greeting is high on the list of voicemail no no's! You sound foolish, and callers wonder what else you might not be doing if you're not updating your greeting. I'd play it safe and not include the date on your greeting.

Which leads us to the message that *you* leave for some-one. It's your electronic business card and it needs to be *great.*

Messages

There are three adjectives that describe the messages you leave: poor, average, and great. The message you leave for someone needs to be *great.* Here's a sample of each. Which one is similar to the type of message you leave?

Poor: Hi, this is Bob. Gimme a call.

Average: Hi, this is Bob at Acme Widgets. Call me at 291-1012. (Said *way* too fast—you know exactly what I'm talking about!)

Great: Hi Nancy. This is Bob Smith at Acme Widgets. I'd like to schedule a time to talk with you about the plan for the meeting on the 27th. I'll plan on having lunch brought in at our office. I'm excited to meet with you on this. My number is 314-291-1012. Again, that's 314-291-1012. If I'm not in, ask for Judy at extension 42 and she can take a message for me. I'm looking forward to our meeting, Nancy. Thanks.

Let's not make using voicemail any more difficult than it really is. It can and should be a productivity enhancer, not a source of frustration.

Now that you've read this, call in to your own voicemail system and listen for how many of these frustrating phrases or practices your company uses...then eliminate them.

Don't forget to call and check your cell phone, too. How does your voicemail greeting sound?

Cell Phone Flubs—
The Dirty Dozen

New phone? Old phone? New number? Home number? Old Number? Whose service? Which service? How many minutes? One phone? Two phones? There are a lot more choices now.

However, along with more choices comes the "same old...same old." Most everyone has a pet peeve about cell phones. To set matters straight, here are the Dirty Dozen Cell Phone Etiquette Flubs from the Telephone Doctor.

1. Using a cell phone in a restaurant, a theater, or other public areas in which others will become annoyed. Take your phone call to a private area. No one needs, or wants, to hear your conversation.

2. Raising your voice. Most cell phone users are not even aware of how much louder they talk while on their cell phone. Go to a quiet corner and cover your mouth.

3. Using a cell phone while driving without the hands-free device. The state of New York and others now have a law in effect prohibiting driving without the hands-free device. More states will follow. It is dangerous. You cannot do two things well at once.

4. Being a show-off. Big deal. You've got a phone. Watch the cell phone users that have their heads on a "spindle." They want to be sure you see them using their cell phones; it makes them feel important. Bad news!

5. Taking an incoming cell phone call while in a situation that should not be interrupted. I was interviewing an applicant when her phone rang. Don't take those calls...or better yet, see #6! This leaves a bad first impression.

6. Leaving your ringer on in those situations where it would disturb others. Silence your phone when at a seminar, movie theater, a religious gathering, the grocery store, and a funeral. (Yes, I've heard horror stories on that, frightening as it is.)

7. Making calls on airplanes. Most of the cell phone calls placed on an airplane sound useless. They go something like this: "Hi, I'm on the plane. We're about to take off—I'll let you know when I land." Then the next call is: "Hello, we've landed—talk with you later." Could this conversation not have waited until the person was in the airport where they could have held an intelligent conversation? However, on the bright side...cell phones are great for when you're stuck in the plane on the tarmac in a holding position. Then, it's even gracious to offer your cell phone to others who may need to let someone know about the delay.

8. Making calls in public bathrooms. This is just simply unnecessary. End of subject.

9. No texting while you're driving either.

10. Walking into an elevator while in the middle of a cell phone conversation. Admittedly it's better than just staring at the numbers as they go from floor-to-floor, but, in truth, your riding companions honestly don't want to get in on your conversation.

11. Making calls at the hair salon. The stylist is not able to cut around the cell phone. Give it a break. You'll be glad when you see the finished product that you waited to make that call.

12. Leaving your cell phone on while at work. Give your job your undivided attention and your coworkers some respect. Wait until your lunch hour or after work, and then use your cell phone.

So where can you use a cell phone comfortably in the Telephone Doctor's opinion? "Really anywhere when used with good common sense and judgment. Take yourself and your cell phone to an area where you're not disturbing others. It's that simple."

Are you a cell phone abuser?

E-mail Errors: Simple Kindness or Common Sense?

The question *used* to be: "Nancy, what do you think of people who don't return their phone calls?" Today we insert the word *e-mail* for *phone calls.*

My answer on not returning phone calls was simple: Not returning a phone call is plain rude. It's like not using your turn signal when switching lanes. With phone calls, you can have someone else return the call on your behalf. You can record a message that tells where you are, when you will return, and who to contact in your absence. Perhaps it's something you can delegate. You merely forward the voicemail to an associate and ask him/her to handle the situation for you.

Well, you know what? It's even easier with e-mail. All you need to do with e-mail is hit REPLY, knock out a few words, and bingo, you're on your way to better e-mail manners.

I am well aware that many of us get way too many e-mails. A client once told me that if there are more than two e-mails on the same subject between two people, it's time for a face-to-face meeting. I agree. How many of us get on the e-mail merry go round, only to have nothing finalized after dozens of interactions, some of which last for days. It also seems to happen more internally than with e-mails received from customers. It's as though the out-of-town or client's e-mail is more important than the internal customers e-mails, so we'll answer the external e-mails first.

E-mails and voicemail are similar in the fact that they involve information sent one-way. They are asynchronous:

193

received and answered at will. This is unlike a phone conversation or face-to-face meeting, which are synchronous. When two people are talking at the same time, you get immediate information and answers.

I digress! Back to not returning e-mails. If you don't want to hear from that company or person again, tell them so. It's done in what Telephone Doctor calls distance-induced bravery. However, please remember that the written word does not have any tone to it. Without a tone, a message can be interpreted differently. Please be sure to add the niceties such as *please, thank you,* and other soft easy words when you're rejecting someone.

A prompt response to e-mails that need answers is key. Certainly if you have one-way information that doesn't need answering, that's all well and good. But when a question is asked, take the time to answer it. If information is needed, take the time to provide it. The fact that an e-mail gets acknowledged is an act of kindness.

A few words on ALL CAPS IN AN E-MAIL: It is often said that using all caps means that you are yelling. And that's right; however, sometimes we want to yell. Like GOOD JOB, Bob. Or I LOVE YOU LOTS! Or THANK YOU SO MUCH FOR THE AWESOME GIFT. Then go back to a normal font. All caps in a positive sense isn't all that bad. RIGHT?

Simple kindness and common sense. Not returning e-mails is as offensive as not returning a phone call.

THANK YOU FOR READING THIS!
(There! I yelled it!)

About the Author

Nancy Friedman is president of Telephone Doctor®, an International customer service training company, based in St. Louis, Missouri. Nancy is a featured speaker at association meetings and corporate gatherings around the world. She has appeared on *OPRAH, The Today Show,* CNN, *Good Morning America,* and *CBS This Morning.* Her articles have been published in the *Wall Street Journal, USA Today,* as well as hundreds of other radio, TV, and print outlets. For more information, log onto the Telephone Doctor® Web site at www.telephonedoctor.com, or call 314-291-1012.